THE BROTHERS KARAMAZOV

NOTES

including
- *Life and Background*
- *General Plot Summary*
- *List of Characters*
- *Summaries and Commentaries*
- *Character Analyses*
- *Chronological Chart*
- *Review Questions*
- *Selected Bibliography*

by
Gary Carey, M.A.
University of Colorado
and
James L. Roberts, Ph.D.
Department of English
University of Nebraska

WILEY

Wiley Publishing, Inc.

Editor

Gary Carey, M.A., University of Colorado

Consulting Editor

James L. Roberts, Ph.D., Department of
English, University of Nebraska

Production

Wiley Publishing, Inc. Composition Services

CliffsNotes™ *The Brothers Karamazov*

Published by:
Wiley Publishing, Inc.
909 Third Avenue
New York, NY 10022
www.wiley.com

CONTENTS

The Brothers Karamazov Notes

LIFE AND BACKGROUND

Fyodor Mikhailovich Dostoevsky was born of lower-middle-class parents in 1821, the second of seven children, and lived until 1881. His father, an army doctor attached to the staff of a public hospital, was a stern and righteous man while his mother was the opposite — passive, kindly, and generous — and this fact accounts perhaps for Dostoevsky's often filling his novels with characters who seem to possess opposite extremes of character.

Dostoevsky's early education was in an army engineering school, where he was apparently bored with the dull routine and the unimaginative student life. He spent most of his time, therefore, dabbling in literary matters and reading the latest authors; the penchant for literature was obsessive. And, almost as obsessive was Dostoevsky's interest in death, for while the young student was away at school, his father was killed by the serfs on his estate. This sudden and savage murder smouldered within the young Dostoevsky and, when he began to write, the subject of crime, and murder in particular, was present in every new publication; Dostoevsky was never free of the horrors of homicide and even at the end of his life, he chose to write of a violent death — the death of a father — as the basis for his masterpiece, *The Brothers Karamazov*.

After spending two years in the army, Dostoevsky launched his literary career with *Poor Folk*, a novel which was an immediate and popular success and one highly acclaimed by the critics. Never before had a Russian author so thoroughly examined the psychological complexity of man's inner feelings and the intricate workings of the mind.

Following *Poor Folk*, Dostoevsky's only important novel for many years was *The Double*, a short work dealing with a split personality and containing the genesis of a later masterpiece, *Crime and Punishment*.

Perhaps the most crucial years of Dostoevsky's melodramatic life occurred soon after the publication of *Poor Folk*. These years included some of the most active, changing phases in all of Russian history and Dostoevsky had an unusually active role in this era of change. Using influences acquired with his literary achievements, he became involved in political intrigues of quite questionable natures. He was, for example, deeply influenced by new and radical ideas entering Russia from the West and soon became affiliated with those who hoped to revolutionize Russia with all sorts of Western reforms. The many articles Dostoevsky wrote, concerning the various political questions, he published knowing full well that they were illegal and that all printing was to be controlled and censored by the government.

The rebel-writer and his friends were, of course, soon deemed treasonous revolutionaries and placed in prison and, after nine months, a number of them, including Dostoevsky, were tried, found guilty, and condemned to be shot by a firing squad.

The entire group was accordingly assembled, all preparations were completed, and the victims were tied and blindfolded. Then, seconds before the shots were to be fired, a messenger from the Tsar arrived. A reprieve had been granted. Actually the Tsar had never intended that the men were to be shot; he merely used this sadistic method to teach Dostoevsky and his friends a lesson. This soul-shaking, harrowing encounter with death, however, created a never-to-be forgotten impression on Dostoevsky; it haunted him for the rest of his life.

After the commutation of the death sentence, Dostoevsky was sent to Siberia and during the years there, he changed his entire outlook on life. During this time, amidst horrible living conditions — stench, ugliness, hardened criminals, and filth — he began to re-examine his values. There was total change within the man. He experienced his first epileptic seizure and he began to reject a heretofore blind acceptance of new ideas which Russia was absorbing. He underwent a spiritual regeneration so profound that he emerged with a prophetic belief in the sacred mission of the Russian people. He believed that the salvation of the world was in the hands of the Russian folk and that eventually Russia would rise to dominate the world. It was also in prison that Dostoevsky formulated his well-known theories about the necessity of suffering. Suffering became the means by which man's soul is purified; it expiated sin; it became man's sole means of salvation.

When Dostoevsky left Siberia, he resumed his literary career and soon became one of the great spokesmen of Russia. Then, in 1866, he published his first masterpiece, *Crime and Punishment*. The novel is the story of Raskolnikov, a university student who commits a senseless murder to test his moral and metaphysical theories concerning the freedom of the will. The novel exhibits all the brilliant psychological analyses of character for which Dostoevsky was to become famous and incorporates the theme of redemption through suffering.

Most of Dostoevsky's adult life was plagued with marital problems, epileptic seizures and, most of all, by creditors. Often he had to compose novels at top speed in order to pay his many mounting debts, but by the end of his life, he was sufficiently free of worry so that he was able to devote all his energy to the composition of *The Brothers Karamazov* and at his death, only a year after the publication of this masterwork, he was universally acknowledged to be one of Russia's greatest writers.

GENERAL PLOT SUMMARY

By his first wife, Fyodor Karamazov sired one son — Dmitri — and by his second wife, two sons — Ivan and Alyosha. None of the Karamazov boys, however, was reared in the family home. Their mothers dead and their father a drunken fornicator, they were parceled out to various relatives. Fyodor could not have been more grateful; he could devote all energy and time to his notorious orgies. Those were the early years.

Dmitri comes of age, as the novel opens, and asks his father for an inheritance which, he has long been told, his mother left him. His request is scoffed at. Old Karamazov feigns ignorance of any mythical monies or properties that are rightfully Dmitri's. The matter is far from ended, though, for Dmitri and his father find themselves instinctive enemies and besides quarreling over the inheritance, they vie for Grushenka, a woman of questionable reputation. Finally it is suggested that if there is to be peace in the Karamazov household that the family must go together to the monastery and allow Alyosha's elder, Father Zossima, to arbitrate and resolve the quarrels. Ivan, Karamazov's intellectual son, accompanies them to the meeting.

At the monastery there seems to be little hope for a successful reconciliation. Fyodor parades his usual disgusting vulgarities, makes a dreadful scene, and when Dmitri arrives late, he accuses his son of all sorts of degeneracy. Dmitri then retorts that his father has tried to lure Grushenka into a liaison by promising her 3,000 rubles, and in the midst of their shouting, Father Zossima bows and kisses Dmitri's feet. This act ends the interview. All are shocked into silence. Later, old Karamazov recovers from his astonishment and once again he makes a disgraceful scene in the dining room of the Father Superior. He then leaves the monastery and commands Alyosha to leave also.

It is now that Dostoevsky reveals that Karamazov perhaps has fathered another son. Years ago, a raggle-taggle moron girl who roamed the town was seduced and bore a child; everyone, naturally, assumed that the satyr-like Karamazov was responsible. The child grew up to be an epileptic and now cooks for Karamazov. He is a strange sort, this Smerdyakov, and lately his epileptic seizures have become more frequent. Curiously, he enjoys talking philosophy with Ivan.

The day after the explosive scene in the monastery, Alyosha comes to visit his father and is stopped midway by Dmitri. The emotional, impulsive Karamazov son explains to Alyosha that he is sick with grief — that some time ago, he became engaged to a girl named Katerina, and has recently borrowed 3,000 rubles from her to finance an orgy with Grushenka. He pleads for Alyosha to speak to Katerina, to break the engagement, and to help him find some way to repay the squandered money so that he can feel free to elope with Grushenka. Alyosha promises to help if he is able.

The young man reaches his father's house and finds more confusion: Smerdyakov is loudly arguing with another servant about religion, spouting many of Ivan's ideas. Later, when the servants are ordered away, Karamazov taunts Ivan and Alyosha about God and immortality, and Ivan answers that he believes in neither. Alyosha quietly affirms the existence of both. Dmitri then bursts into the room crying for Grushenka and when he cannot find her, attacks his father and threatens to kill him.

Alyosha tends his father's wounds, then goes back to the monastery for the night. The next day he goes to see Katerina, as he promised Dmitri, and tries to convince her that she and Ivan love each other and that she should not concern herself with Dmitri and his problems. He is unsuccessful.

Later that same day, Alyosha comes upon Ivan in a restaurant, and they continue the conversation about God and immortality that they began at their father's house. Ivan says that he cannot accept a world in which God allows so many innocent people to suffer and Alyosha says that, although Ivan cannot comprehend the logic of God, there is One who can comprehend all: Jesus. Ivan then explains, with his poem "The Grand Inquisitor," that Jesus is neither a ready nor an easy answer-all for his questionings — that He placed an intolerable burden on man by giving him total freedom of choice.

When Alyosha returns to the monastery, he finds Father Zossima near death. The elder rallies a bit and lives long enough to expound his religious beliefs to his small audience, stressing, above all, a life of simplicity, a life in which every man shall love all people and all things, and shall refrain from condemning others. This is Zossima's final wisdom and when he finishes, he dies.

Next day many people gather to view the holy man's corpse, for popular rumor has whispered for years that upon Zossima's death, a miracle would occur. No miracle occurs, however. Instead, a foul and putrid odor fills the room and all of the mourners are horrified. Even Alyosha questions God's justice and, momentarily yielding to temptation, he flees to Grushenka's house. But after he has talked with the girl, he discovers that she is not the sinful woman he sought; she is remarkably sensitive and quite understanding and compassionate. Alyosha's faith is restored and, later, in a dream of Jesus' coming to the wedding of Cana, he realizes that life is meant to be joyously shared. Now he is absolutely certain of his faith in God and in immortality.

Dmitri has meanwhile been frantically searching for a way to raise the money to repay Katerina. He has even gone to a neighboring town to try and borrow the sum, but even there he fails. Returning, he discovers that Grushenka is no longer at home and panics, sure that she has succumbed to Fyodor's rubles. He goes first to his father's house; then, after discovering that she is not there, he tries to escape but is cornered by an old servant. He strikes him aside, leaving him bloody and unconscious, and returns to Grushenka's house. He demands to know her whereabouts and at last he is told that she has gone to join a former lover, one who deserted her five years before.

Dmitri makes a final decision: he will see Grushenka once more, for the last time, then kill himself. He travels to the couple's rendezvous, finds Grushenka celebrating with her lover, and joins them. There is resentment and arguing, and finally Grushenka is convinced that her former lover is a scoundrel and that it is Dmitri whom she really loves. The two lovers are not to be reunited, however, for the police arrive and accuse Dmitri of murdering his father. Both are stunned by the circumstantial evidence, for the accusation is weighty. Dmitri indeed seems guilty and is indicted to stand trial.

Alyosha, in the meantime, has made friends with a young schoolboy, the son of a man brutally beaten by Dmitri in a rage of passion and gradually the youth has proven his sincere desire to help the frightened, avenging boy. Now that the youngster is dying, Alyosha remains at his bedside, where he hopes to help the family and also to reconcile the young boy with many of his schoolmates.

Ivan, the intellectual, has neither the romantic passion of Dmitri nor the wide, spiritual interests of Alyosha, and when he learns of his father's murder, he broods, then decides to discuss his theories with Smerdyakov. He is astonished at the bastard servant's open confession that he is responsible for the murder. But Smerdyakov is clever; he disavows total responsibility and maintains that Ivan gave him the intellectual and moral justification for the murder and, furthermore, that he actually permitted the act by leaving town so that Smerdyakov would be free to accomplish the deed. Ivan is slow to accept the argument but after he does, he is absolutely convinced of Smerdyakov's logic. The transition is disastrous. His newfound guilt makes him a madman and the night before Dmitri's trial, he is devoured with burning brain fever. That same night Smerdyakov commits suicide. Dmitri's situation becomes increasingly perilous.

During the trial, the circumstantial evidence is presented in so thorough a manner that Dmitri is logically convicted as Fyodor's murderer. He has the motive, the passion, and was at the scene of the crime. Perhaps the most damning bit of evidence, however, is presented by Katerina. She shows the court a letter of Dmitri's in which he says that he fears that he might be driven to murder his father.

After the conviction, Dmitri agrees to certain plans for his escape but says that it will be great torture and suffering for him to flee from Mother Russia, from Russian soil, and to live in exile.

As for Alyosha, his future holds the promise of hope and goodness (qualities that were once never associated with the Karamazovs), for after young Ilusha dies and all his schoolmates attend the funeral, Alyosha gathers them together and deeply impresses them with his explanation of love and of friendship. Spontaneously, the boys rise and cheer Alyosha and his wisdom.

LIST OF CHARACTERS

KARAMAZOV FAMILY

Fyodor Pavlovitch Karamazov

The father, who is a cynical, immoral, and depraved sensualist dedicated only to the fulfillment of his carnal desires.

Dmitri (Mitya)

His oldest son, who develops an intense hatred for his father and who is convicted of murdering him.

Ivan

The second son, who develops into the extreme intellectual and who questions all values of life.

Alyosha (Alexey)

The youngest son, who is deeply religious and who functions as the central figure in the novel.

Smerdyakov (Pavel Fyodorovitch Smerdyakov)

Old Karamazov's illegitimate son, whose last name was assigned to him by Fyodor and whose first names were merely adopted. He grows up in the Karamazov house as a servant.

Adelaida

Karamazov's first wife and the mother of Dmitri.

Sofya

Karamazov's second wife and the mother of Ivan and Alyosha.

OTHER CHARACTERS

Andrey

The driver who takes Dmitri to his meeting with Grushenka in Mokroe.

Trifon Borissovitch

The innkeeper at Mokroe who testifies that Dmitri spent all of the three thousand rubles during his orgy.

Fenya

Grushenka's maid, who lies to Dmitri about Grushenka's whereabouts.

Father Ferapont

The acetic and deranged monk who is a bitter opponent to Father Zossima.

Fetyukovitch

The brilliant defense attorney brought in from Moscow to defend Dmitri.

Gorstkin (also known as Lyagavy)

The merchant who is interested in buying some property belonging to Karamazov.

Grigory Vassilyevitch

The old Karamazov servant who takes care of the children and who adopts Smerdyakov.

Grushenka (Agrafena Alexandrovna)

The lady of so-called loose morals who attracts the attentions and consequent jealousies of Dmitri and Fyodor.

Herzenstube

The old town doctor who gives favorable testimony in Dmitri's behalf.

Madame Hohlakov

The wealthy widow at whose house many of the scenes of the novel take place.

Lise

Madame Hohlakov's young daughter, who becomes engaged to Alyosha and then capriciously breaks the engagement.

Ilusha

The young boy whose illness brings all of his friends together with Alyosha.

Father Iosif (Joseph)

The librarian at the monastery.

Kalganov (Pyotr Fomitch Kalganov)

A casual friend who is present at Dmitri's party in Mokroe.

Katerina (Katya) Ivanovna

Dmitri's fiancée, whom he deserts upon falling in love with Grushenka.

Ippolit Kirillovitch

The public prosecutor who conducts the trial against Dmitri.

Kolya (Nikolay Ivanovitch Krassotkin)

The young boy who influences the other boys and becomes Alyosha's disciple.

Madame Krassotkin (Anna Fyodorovna)

Kolya's doting and widowed mother.

Lizaveta Smerdyastchaya

The town's deformed idiot, who is seduced by Karamazov and then gives birth to Smerdyakov.

Lyagavy

See *Gorstkin*.

Makarov (Mihail Makarovitch Makarov)

The district police inspector who questions Dmitri about the murder.

Marfa Ignatyevna

Grigory's wife and another of the Karamazov servants.

Marya Kondratyevna

The daughter of Dmitri's landlady who is in love with Smerdyakov.

Maximov

An old destitute landowner who lives off the generosity of others, especially Grushenka, in the closing chapters of the novel.

Miusov (Pyotr Alexandrovitch Miusov)

A cousin of Karamazov's first wife, who was instrumental in having Dmitri taken away from Fyodor.

Mussyalovitch

Grushenka's ex-lover, whose return precipitated Dmitri's strange behavior on the night of the murder.

Father Paissy

The learned theologian and devoted friend of Father Zossima who tries to console Alyosha.

Pyotr Ilyitch Perhotin

The young civil servant from whom Dmitri borrowed money on the night of the murder.

Mihail Ospovitch Rakitin

A young seminarian who professes to have very liberal and advanced ideas and who betrays his friendship with Alyosha.

Samsonov (Kuzma Samsonov)

A wealthy landowner who befriended Grushenka.

Captain Snegiryov

Ilusha's father, who is destitute and broken by misfortunes. He was attacked by Dmitri one night because he earned money from Fyodor.

Varvinsky

A district doctor who testifies as to Dmitri's mental condition.

Vrublevsky

Mussyalovitch's companion on the night of the orgy in Mokroe.

Father Zossima

The revered elder at the monastery and the spiritual guardian for Alyosha, whose teachings become central to all the ideas in the novel.

SUMMARIES AND COMMENTARIES

PART ONE

BOOK I

Summary

Karamazov: the name is well-known in Russia; it carries a taste of violence and dark Slavic passion. And there is much truth in the rumors and whispered tales told of Fyodor Karamazov. In his youth he was a loud profligate. His drinking and high living were notorious; he seemed insatiate. And marriage did not tame him. His marriage, true to form, was scandalous. But initially it was not scandalous because of its melodramatic elements — that was to be expected; life with Karamozov could not be otherwise. Initially, Karamazov's marriage was scandalous because it was romantic: he was penniless yet he wooed and married an heiress.

Adelaida Ivanovna believed in her young rebel-husband. Perhaps his spirit was bold and irrepressible, but he was the new breed of liberal Russian manhood. She believed it firmly. She tried to believe it for a long time. Then she was forced to face the ugly reality that instead of a rich-blooded idealist she had married an opportunist who was physically cruel and usually drunk. She also was forced to face another unpleasant truth: she was pregnant. She bore the baby, a son — Dmitri, or Mitya as she often called him — and when she could no longer endure her husband's viciousness, she abandoned both her son and husband and eloped with a young student.

Karamazov, ostensibly, was staggered by her rejection and, still the overly dramatic sort, like a loud tragedian he spent many of his days driving through the country, lamenting over his wife's desertion. But even that pose grew wearisome and soon he returned to his life of debauchery. When he received the news of Adelaida's death he was in the midst of a drunken orgy.

Young Dmitri was neglected and finally taken in by a cousin and when the cousin tired of him the child was given to other relatives; thus the baby grew up with a variety of families. But he was always told about his real father, that the man still lived, and that he held a rather large piece of Adelaida's property that was rightfully Dmitri's. The boy never forgot these tales of land and money and when he reached maturity, he visited his father and asked about the inheritance. He was unable, of course, to get any information from the old man but he began receiving small sums of money and, convinced that the property did exist, he revisited his father. Again the old man evaded his son's questions.

But if Karamazov was able to evade Dmitri, he could not evade other matters so successfully — the problems of his other sons, for example. For after the four-year-old Dmitri was taken away, Karamazov married a second time. This wife, Sofya Ivanovna, was remarkably beautiful and her loveliness and her innocence attracted the lustful Karamazov. He convinced her to elope with him against her guardian's wishes and quickly took advantage of her meekness. He began having loose women in the house and even carried on orgies of debauchery in her presence.

During Karamazov's years of cruelty and depravity, Sofya Ivanovna gave birth to two sons, Ivan and Alyosha. But she was not well and did not feel loved despite the attentions of old Grigory, the servant who did his best to comfort her and protect her from Karamazov. In spite of his care, she soon fell ill and died. When her former guardian heard about her death, she came and took the two boys, Ivan and Alyosha, with her and upon her own death she left a thousand rubles to each boy for his education.

Ivan Karamazov developed into a brilliant student who helped support himself by writing for journals and he slowly began to make a name for himself in literary circles. One of his articles, for instance, dealt with the function of the ecclesiastical courts; it attracted widespread interest and even the monastery in his native town spoke of it. Alyosha, the youngest Karamazov, developed into a devoutly religious person, his faith based on reality and untinged by mysticism or fanaticism. He was universally well liked, never criticized anyone, and seemed to love everyone.

As the action of the novel begins, Alyosha returns to his father's house and meets his brothers. He and Dmitri rapidly become good friends, but he feels puzzled by Ivan's reserve and intellectuality. As for his father, Alyosha openly loves him; he has never criticized or condemned his father's way of life. Alyosha has always been generous and forgiving, thus it was that Karamazov was not surprised when Alyosha first told him that he wanted to become a monk, the disciple of the renowned elder, Zossima. In those days, incidentally, an elder was often controversial. "An elder," it was said, "was one who took your soul, your will, into his soul and his will." But elder, by also setting exemplary models of holiness in their own lives, often attracted large numbers of followers.

The Karamazovs are reunited and the reason for their reunion deeply concerns Alyosha. The discord between Dmitri and his father has reached such a point that one of them, apparently the father, has suggested a meeting in Father Zossima's cell, where they can discuss differences under the conciliating influence of the elder. Alyosha, who understands his brothers and his father better than most people think, greatly fears the meeting.

Commentary

The Brothers Karamazov is often considered one of the world's most complex novels. Dostoevsky examines many different facets of life, investigates many problems of lasting importance, and is able to do so successfully in this novel because the mere size and bulk of the book allows him to proceed with deliberate slowness in introducing and in developing his ideas. Attempting in these Commentaries, however, to isolate some of the main ideas and to analyze them, destroys the essential unity of the novel. Part of its greatness is the manner in which Dostoevsky is able to integrate all the divergent elements into one unified whole. Each idea borders upon another and is somewhat vitiated when isolated from the remainder of the novel.

In the complex spirit of the novel and in the leisurely nineteenth-century fashion of giving the intricate background of the main characters, Dostoevsky begins his book, then immediately establishes its tone. He first announces the element of mystery in the novel — the "gloomy and tragic death" of Karamazov — then begins defining the elements of tragedy — especially, the Karamazov tragedy.

The older Karamazov is depicted as base, vulgar, ill-natured, and completely degraded and his "tragic" death will be revealed to be tragic only because his sons are implicated in the death — not because Karamazov himself arouses tragic emotion. In fact, in the trial scene later in the book, it is pointed out that the murder is not a parricide in the truest sense because Fyodor Karamazov never has functioned as a proper father. And, to support this idea, Dostoevsky begins at the very outset of the novel to show the blackness and vulgarity of the man who is to be murdered.

To emphasize the monster within Karamazov, Dostoevsky illustrates the lack of any paternal instincts. Karamazov did not discard his children from hatred or malice; he simply forgot about their existence. Furthermore, he was pleased each time that strangers came and took the children and therefore released him from responsibility; this allowed him to devote all his energy to his various orgies. One of Dostoevsky's ideas, prominent throughout the novel, then, concerns the place of the child in society and this theme receives its first expression in the chapter dealing with Fyodor Karamazov's treatment of his children.

In Chapter 2, Dostoevsky tells us that Dmitri "was the only one of Fyodor Pavlovitch's three sons who grew up in the belief that he had property and that he would be independent on coming of age." This idea is established early in the novel because it becomes the source of the antagonism existing between father and son. Dostoevsky carefully avoids making a direct statement about the full extent to which the father has cheated his son, but by the manner in which he arranges his descriptions of the father, we can assume that Fyodor has indeed cheated Dmitri out of a major portion of the inheritance. It is also noteworthy that of the three sons Dmitri is the only one whom the father intensely dislikes. This is easily explained: the other two sons make no financial demands upon the father; only Dmitri insists upon having his inheritance.

Following his thorough characterization of the older Karamazov, Dostoevsky devotes the next several chapters to the offspring — the brothers Karamazov, as different from one another as can be imagined.

Dmitri, throughout the novel, develops into the extreme sensualist, the emotional son. He did not complete his education; instead, he worked his way up through the military ranks to become an officer. He lacked discipline, however, and soon became involved in a duel and was demoted. Later he gained promotion again. But his deeds and emotions are fluid and fluctuating. He has, for instance, an instinctive dislike for his father but forms an immediate friendship with his brother Alyosha. He is the fiery-hearted, fierce, and emotional person who is easily swayed by his feelings.

Ivan, on the other hand, is the cold intellectual. At an early age he developed his propensity for study and his unusual aptitude for learning. He is the very proud son, always conscious that his early training was at someone else's expense. He began, therefore, as soon as possible, to write reviews in order to support himself, and before arriving in his native town, he has published a widely read, widely discussed article about the ecclesiastical courts. This article is the subject of a conversation in the next book between the monks and Ivan.

In contrast to his two brothers, Alyosha has none of Ivan's pride, nor is he as fiery as Dmitri. He is "simply an early lover of humanity," one who always tries to see the best side of everyone. He possesses an implicit trust in all people and, in all his relationships, he never judges others. Beneath his modest exterior, however, is a penetrating and understanding mind that detects many subtleties and distinctions. Alyosha is of course deeply religious but he is not the fanatical sort who bases his faith upon miracles. He is the complete realist who arrived at his beliefs concerning immortality and God through reasoning.

While presenting the characteristics of the three Karamazov sons, Dostoevsky introduces another principal theme — the conflict between faith and disbelief. Alyosha and Ivan represent the two opposite poles of acceptance and it is only natural that they do not become intimate friends at first. Alyosha, however, is perceptive enough to understand Ivan's problem. He knows that "Ivan was absorbed in something — something inward and important that he was striving toward, some goal, perhaps very hard to attain and that was why he had no thought for him." Looking forward, we realize that Ivan will forever struggle with the idea of belief and immortality and that this struggle will form one of the most dramatic sections of the novel. In contrast, Dmitri will slowly become a person of faith. He and Alyosha, consequently, become intimate friends from the very beginning.

In all his writing, Dostoevsky was interested in the psychology of actions. Particularly he was interested in the nature of contradictory actions. Many of his characters therefore perform actions that do not seem consistent with their personalities. Dostoevsky often investigates this idea in an attempt to understand why a person who acts in a certain manner will often perform an action that seemingly contradicts his nature. In the character of the father, for example, he shows Fyodor visiting the grave of his first wife and being so touched by her memory that he gives a thousand rubles to the monastery for requiems. For a man usually so miserly with money and not professing a belief in God, this action is strange and contradictory. Dostoevsky comments that "strange impulses of sudden feeling and sudden thought are common in such types." Later he also writes that Fyodor "was wicked and sentimental," and, even though the question of contradictory actions is never solved by Dostoevsky, it does occupy portions of the novel and the reader should be aware of the investigation.

The introduction of Zossima concludes the first book, the brief introduction being a transitional device. Zossima, one should be aware, will hold stage center in the following section. His role is important because he is antithetical to all but one of the vigorous Karamazov clan. He is a passive sort, yet he influences the decisive actions of Alyosha and thus influences the course of the novel. Dostoevsky attempts, in the character of the elder, to present the almost perfect person, and his characterization is convincing. So convincing, in fact, is it to Alyosha that his beliefs are shaken at Zossima's death. He has convinced himself that after the elder's death Zossima would bring extraordinary glory to the monastery. Death is rarely that simple. The fact that Zossima decomposes so rapidly weighs heavily on Alyosha and he is tempted to question, therefore, the validity of God's justice.

BOOK II

Chapters 1-4

Summary

On the day scheduled for the meeting between the Karamazovs and the elder, Zossima, Fyodor and Ivan arrive accompanied by a former guardian of Dmitri's, Miusov, and a relative of Miusov's, Kalganov. Dmitri Karamazov, however, is not at the monastery and all wonder, naturally, if he will come; he was certainly notified only the previous day. The meeting takes on a certain air of mystery.

A very old monk emerges, greets the guests, then leads them to Father Zossima's cell. All are invited to have lunch with the Father Superior following the interview, he says. First, however, they must wait for Zossima.

The wait, though not long, seems interminable for Miusov. Uncontrollably, he finds himself growing increasingly irritated at the crude jokes that Fyodor Karamazov unleashes concerning the monastic life.

Father Zossima at last arrives, accompanied by Alyosha, two other monks, and Rakitin, a divinity student living under the protection of the monastery. The monks bow and kiss Zossima's hand and receive his blessings; the guests, however, merely bow politely to the elder. Deeply embarrassed by his family's austerity, Alyosha trembles. Now, more than ever, he fears that the meeting will be calamitous.

Karamazov apologizes for Dmitri's absence, then nervously begins a non-stop monolog of coarse anecdotes. At this, Alyosha is even more deeply embarrassed; in fact, everyone except the elder is distressed. The tension mounts and when Karamazov falls climactically to his knees and begs the elder, "what must I do to gain eternal life?" it is difficult to tell whether or not he is still playing the loud-mouth clown. No one but Zossima dares speak. The elder tells Karamazov that he must cease lying and, above all, he must cease lying to himself. At first, Fyodor is impressed by the advice but then resumes his joking and clowning until Zossima excuses himself. He must meet with an assembly of people outside the monastery.

The group outside are all peasant women — all but two. At one side, in a section reserved for the wealthy, are Madame Hohlakov and her partially paralyzed daughter, Lise, waiting to be blessed by the elder and to receive his advice on their problems. Zossima moves among the peasant women listening to their problems and offering them advice, emphasizing always the healing effect of the love of God. "Love is such a priceless treasure," he says, "that you can redeem the world by it and expiate not only your own sins but the sins of others."

Madame Hohlakov confesses to Zossima that, for her part, she suffers from a lack of faith; she can grasp neither the Christian idea of immortality nor any type of life beyond the grave. She says furthermore that if she does a charitable act that she wants to receive thanks and praise for it. Zossima tells her that if she practices active, honest love that she will grow to understand the reality of God and the immortality of her soul. "Attain to perfect self-forgetfulness in the love of your neighbor," he counsels her, "then you will believe without doubt." Ending the interview, he promises her that he will send Alyosha to visit Lise.

Commentary

Book II is largely devoted to a study of Zossima and his teachings. This saintly ascetic influences all of Alyosha's actions and to thoroughly understand this youngest member of the Karamazov clan, one must understand the man to whom he zealously attaches himself.

Zossima seems to have come to terms with life; he lives with perfect contentment and understanding — basically, a quiet and reserved man. He is not, for instance, visibly disturbed by Fyodor Karamazov's buffoonery; his quiet mien allows him to see deeply into the personality of Karamazov — of any person with whom he speaks. With Karamazov, he knows that the old man is intentionally trying to overact, to clown and, later, with Madame Hohlakov, he knows that she makes her confession in order to gain his personal approbation for her frankness. A large part of Father Zossima's greatness, therefore, is this perceptive understanding of mankind, his comprehension of the psychological factors and motivations that prompt human actions; his advice is therefore unusually sound.

Zossima's dignity is unique and, coupled with his extreme humility, most readily impresses a visitor. Alyosha, in contrast, is embarrassed when the Karamazovs do not ask for the elder's blessing, but Zossima shows no outward concern. He merely asks his guests to conduct themselves naturally and to be comfortable; their lack of reverence and discretion in no way offends him. His wisdom encompasses all aspects of life.

In general, Zossima's philosophy is based on the positive rather than on the negative. This is not immediately evident, however, for he tells Karamazov, in terms of negatives, to avoid drunkenness and incontinence, to defy sensual lust, and to realistically value the ruble. But Zossima also offers Karamazov a thoroughly positive view of living, the very simplicity of which should not mislead the reader into thinking that Dostoevsky is being oversimple. Extreme simplicity, in fact, is the key to Zossima's way of life. His is a philosophy founded on a simplicity so basic that it consists of only two concepts: the value of loving and the value of being honest and respecting oneself.

Zossima tells Fyodor, "Above all, don't lie to yourself. The man who lies to himself and listens to his own lie eventually comes to such a pass that he neither distinguishes the truth within him nor around him and so loses all respect for himself and for others." Later, he tells Madame Hohlakov that she cannot be helped so long as she speaks only to impress. "Above all," he says to her, "avoid falsehood, every kind of falsehood, especially to yourself." Zossima is convinced that if man is completely honest with himself, he can evaluate the evils within himself and overcome all such propensities, but when a person is dishonest, he is unable to detect good and righteous impulses; as a consequence, such a man ceases to have any respect for himself and begins, like Karamazov, to play the part of a ridiculous clown. In time such a man will lose all dignity. He will be of no value to himself or to others.

The high premium Zossima places on love is at the heart of this philosophy concerning honesty. When a person ceases to respect himself, he also ceases to love; he "sinks to bestiality in passions and coarse pleasures." Only through love, Zossima believes, can man gain the much-sought-after peace that makes life vibrant. This is essentially Zossima's message to the peasant women. He sends them home with the admonition that "love is such a priceless treasure that you can redeem the whole world by it and expiate not only your own sins but the sins of others." To Madame Hohlakov, who has trouble understanding the concept of immortality, he says, "by the experience of active love" man can be convinced of an afterlife — "strive to love your neighbor actively and indefatigably. In as far as you advance in love you will grow surer of the reality of God and of the immortality of your soul." If a person, he concludes, devotes himself completely to love — love of God, love of the individual—then that man can learn to believe in immortality without doubts.

While such summary statements of Zossima's views seem, on the surface, to be simple, they echo in a large degree the teachings of Jesus and the concepts by which Alyosha tries to live. Throughout the remainder of the novel, Alyosha attempts to practice Zossima's concept of love; he responds lovingly to every character and possesses no animosity for any—not for the small children who ridicule him nor even for Lise, who delights in tormenting him. Moreover, Zossima knows that Alyosha is the one person who can put into practice all of his teachings. And, as the elder sees that Katerina has sent a note for Alyosha and that Lise needs him to come visit her, it is such requests as these that support his decision to send Alyosha to live in the world rather than in the cloister.

Chapters 5-8

Summary

When Father Zossima and Alyosha return to the elder's cell, Ivan is discussing, with two of the monks, his article on the position of the ecclesiastical courts. He explains that he opposes the separation of church and state primarily because when a criminal needs to be punished, the public should not have to rely on the state to administer such punishment. Ivan states that if the church had the authority to punish and also to excommunicate the criminal, then a vast number of crimes would be diminished. To a degree, Father Zossima agrees but he points out that the only effective punishment "lies in the recognition of sin by conscience." According to the elder, the church has no real authority to punish the criminal and, therefore, withdraws "of her own accord" and relies upon "the power of moral condemnation." The discussion continues but is interrupted as Dmitri unexpectedly bursts into the cell.

Breathless, the overwrought Karamazov apologizes for being late, explaining that he was incorrectly informed of the time. He then goes forward, receives Father Zossima's blessing, and sits quietly in the background. As the discussion resumes, Ivan begins to detail his views on immortality and virtue, but is interrupted by Miusov, who scoffs at Ivan's hypothesis that if immortality does not exist then there can be no reason for virtue in the world. Dmitri is deeply disturbed by his brother's theory, especially by his suggesting that without immortality any crime could be committed without fear.

When Ivan and the monks grow quiet, Fyodor nervously resumes his crude verbal antics, then begins to insult Dmitri. In particular, he accuses him of duplicity in his relationships with Katerina Ivanovna and also with Grushenka, an unconventional young woman. Dmitri snaps that Fyodor is only being nasty because he is jealous; he too is infatuated with Grushenka! As the argument mounts and everyone grows more dreadfully embarrassed, Father Zossima suddenly rises from his place and kneels at Dmitri's feet. Then, without uttering a word, he retires to his cell. Everyone is confused as to the meaning of this mysterious act and they comment upon it as they leave the elder's cell to join the Father Superior for lunch. But there is one who cannot remain with the party. Fyodor explains that he is far too embarrassed to accompany them; he says that he is going home.

Alyosha accompanies Father Zossima to his cell and is told by the Father that he must leave the monastery. It is the elder's wish that the young Karamazov rejoin the world. Alyosha does not understand Zossima's request; he desires especially to remain in the monastery — most of all because he knows that Zossima is seriously ill. He desires, as long as possible, to be near the elder.

On the way to the Father Superior's house, Alyosha and Rakitin discuss Zossima's reverent bow before Dmitri. The seminarist says that the bow means that the elder has sensed that the Karamazov house will soon be bathed in blood. The bow, he says, will be remembered and people will say that Zossima foresaw the tragedy for the family. Rakitin continues, tossing out disparaging remarks about the Karamazovs, and teasing Alyosha about Grushenka's designs on him. Alyosha, unaware of Rakitin's motives, innocently refers to Grushenka as one of Rakitin's relatives, and is surprised when the young seminarist becomes highly indignant and loudly denies such relationship.

Meanwhile, Fyodor has changed his mind about attending the luncheon. He returns and unleashes his vicious temper on all present. He delivers a vulgar tirade about the immorality and the hypocrisy of the monks and elders, making the most absurd and ridiculous charges he can conjure up. Ivan finally manages to get the old man in a carriage but the father is not yet subdued. As they are leaving he shouts to Alyosha and orders him to leave the monastery.

Commentary

In a novel of ideas, the views of a certain character will often indicate the deep, essential quality of the personality far more thoroughly than any other device that an author might use. In these chapters, for instance, Ivan's character is revealed through his ideas, especially his views concerning the ecclesiastical courts and the relationship between church and state.

Ivan, unlike many people, does not believe in the separation of church and state on the grounds that the church has no business dealing with criminals. Ivan is, in fact, an unbeliever in the Christian sense but, as a practical matter, he believes that the vast amount of crime in Russia can be curbed by a simple solution. He believes that the state should use the church as a tool in all criminal procedures. Criminals have altogether too easy a lot, he believes. The criminal who steals, for instance, does not feel that he is committing a crime against the church when he steals because the church does not punish him. But, were the church incorporated into the state, any crime would be, besides against the state, automatically against the church. If a potential criminal were threatened with excommunication then crime would virtually be nonexistent.

Besides his views on church and state, Ivan also greatly stresses the power of immortality; without it, there would be no need for man to behave virtuously. Without the matter of immortality, man could commit any crime with no fear of eternal punishment. A belief in immortality, consequently, acts as a deterrent for the potential criminal and restrains him from committing crimes against society that otherwise he would have no compunction about committing. Such extreme views are central to many of Ivan's later struggles and they will have to be reconciled with new concepts following the death of old Karamazov.

After Ivan finishes, Father Zossima, who does not argue with him, penetrates into Ivan's inner self and senses that Ivan is indeed troubled about the problem of faith. The elder is aware that perhaps Ivan does not even know whether or not he actually disbelieves in immortality; perhaps he is only being ironic. This penetrating insight on the part of Father Zossima again attests to his unusual understanding of human nature. Later, of course, it develops that Ivan's madness results from his dilemma over belief and disbelief.

Earlier in the novel Father Zossima's humanity and his simple faith in the healing power of love were stressed. Now, another dimension is added. In these chapters we see that he can easily maintain an intellectual argument. He is no simple mystic; he has an active, alert mind that proves to be a deft opponent for Ivan's parryings. Also, Father Zossima's view of the criminal buttresses his earlier concepts of the power of love. He feels that the worst punishment for a criminal lies in what he calls the "recognition of sin by conscience." The state, according to him, can punish the criminal, but physical punishment does not reform a man nor does it deter future crime. A criminal must realize that crime is a wrongdoing by a son of a Christian society. Only in this realization can a criminal be deterred.

Father Zossima's deep understanding of human nature is recognized by Ivan, for after their discussion, he goes forward to receive the elder's blessings. When he came to the cell, remember, he did not go forward to either greet the elder or to receive a blessing.

The much-discussed bow of Zossima can be explained as being a part of his instinctive understanding of Dmitri's nature. He knows that Dmitri will suffer immeasurably but that his basic nature is honorable. Also, remember that unlike the others, Dmitri arrived and immediately went forward to receive a blessing from the Father. Zossima noted the act and later was keenly aware of Dmitri's dismay when he heard Ivan's theory on immortality and its relation to crime. In Dmitri, Zossima sees great love, great suffering, and ultimately, a great redemption.

Karamazov's flagrantly vulgar behavior is best explained in terms of Dostoevsky's purpose. The author is creating a portrait of a totally repulsive profligate for whom one can feel no sympathy. In this way Dostoevsky alleviates much of the horror that might otherwise accompany the murder.

In this book we are given our first reports about Grushenka. We hear, for example, that she is brazen enough to openly say that she hopes to devour young Alyosha. These reports, however, are hearsay; they vary from the character whom we eventually meet.

BOOK III

Chapters 1-5

Summary

Long ago a child with six fingers was born to Grigory and Marfa, Karamazov's servants; it lived only two weeks but was immediately replaced by a foundling, discovered under rather curious circumstances. On the night of his baby's burial, Grigory thought that he heard an infant crying in the yard. He investigated and found a dying young girl and, lying beside her, a newborn child. The mother was an idiot girl, commonly known as "stinking Lizaveta." But in spite of her abominable appellation, almost everyone liked the harmless feebleminded waif; many even provided her with food and clothing. Lizavetta grew up like the town's stray pet and, naturally, the townspeople were outraged when it was discovered that she was pregnant. It was unthinkable that someone would molest a helpless idiot, a girl who could not even talk —could not even identify her seducer. Rumors as to the father's identity, however, finally agreed on a culprit: old Karamazov. The baby, meanwhile, was adopted by Grigory and Marfa, and they called it by the name Karamazov assigned to it: Smerdyakov.

After Alyosha leaves the monastery, he finds himself growing increasingly fearful of his interview with Katerina Ivanovna, even though he knows that the girl is trying to save Dmitri from disgrace. But he has promised to see her, so he departs. He takes a shortcut to Katerina's house and is stopped by Dmitri. His brother insists upon talking, explaining that he can tell only Alyosha everything that troubles him. Immediately he begins an anguished confession of his baseness and sensuality. Painfully he recounts his history and particularly he ponders over this quirk in his sordidness: whenever he is in the very depths of degradation, he says, he likes to sing Schiller's "Hymn to Joy." He tells Alyosha of his irresponsible life as an army officer and describes his first encounter with Katerina Ivanovna. Then, she was the proud and beautiful daughter of the commanding officer of the camp and, for some time, she ignored Dmitri's presence and remained at a proper distance. But when Dmitri secretly discovered that her father had lent 4,500 rubles to a scoundrel who refused to pay them back, he sent a message saying that her father was about to be arrested. He would, though, lend her the money if she would, as payment, come to his room. He hoped to use the promise of a loan to seduce the proud and beautiful Katerina.

When Katerina arrived, Dmitri suddenly changed. He felt like such a blackguard before the frightened and beautiful girl that he gave her the money without trying to take advantage of her. She bowed down to the floor, then ran away. And, sometime later, after her father died, she came into a large inheritance from a distant relative. She returned the money and offered to marry Dmitri. He agreed and such were, he explains to Alyosha, the circumstances of the engagement.

Following his engagement, Dmitri returned to his father's town and became madly infatuated with Grushenka. But, though she heard much of the gossip about Dmitri, Katerina remained faithful and devoted to him. On one occasion, she even trusted him with 3,000 rubles to send to her half-sister; characteristically, Dmitri squandered the money on an all-night revel. His companion that night was Grushenka.

Now, Dmitri can no longer endure the burden of Katerina's love. He asks Alyosha to be understanding and to go to Katerina and break the engagement. He also has one other request of his brother: he asks him to go to their father and ask for enough money to repay Katerina the 3,000 rubles. The money exists, Dmitri assures Alyosha; he knows for a fact that Fyodor has 3,000 rubles in an envelope intended for Grushenka if ever she spends one night with him. If Alyosha will do this, Dmitri swears that he will repay Katerina and never again ask for money.

Commentary

In the opening chapter of this section, we receive much information about the Karamazov servants. Dostoevsky is not being needlessly thorough; these servants will play a significant role in the murder of old Karamazov and it is well that we become acquainted with them early in the novel. We learn that Grigory was a determined and an obstinate man, for example. "If once he had been brought by any reasons to believe that it [his viewpoint] was immutably right," Dostoevsky tells us, "then nothing can make him change his mind." Consequently, some of the damaging evidence at Dmitri's trial is given by this old servant, a man who would never change his story even though the reader knows that the servant's evidence is false.

Besides the character of Grigory, Dostoevsky also deals with the relationship between Alyosha and his father. "Alyosha," he says, "brought with him something his father had never known before: a complete absence of contempt for him and an invariable kindness, a perfectly natural unaffected devotion to the old man who deserved it so little." We, of course, understand that Alyosha is only following the dictates of Father Zossima, who advocates that one must love indiscriminately, even those who do evil to us.

Also dealt with in this section is one more highly individual character in this Karamazov tangle of personalities — the village idiot, "stinking Lizaveta," whose depiction grandly displays Dostoevsky's greatness in capturing the essentials that round out and animate his cast of minor characters. Here, in a few sure strokes, he creates a grotesque to whom we respond as a human being. Lizaveta is strikingly real; we believe in this creature who sleeps in barns and in passageways and whose appearance is so repulsive that some people are actually appalled. And, we learn that it was Karamazov who fathered her child; now all of his noxious qualities suddenly become putrescent. To dare think that anyone might embrace her is shocking, but to think Karamazov satisfied his lust upon her is to equate him with a barbaric and sordid savage; the man is bestial. He later tells Ivan and Alyosha that "there are no ugly women. The fact that she is a woman is half the battle."

Smerdyakov, then, the fourth son of Fyodor Karamazov, is the offspring of an idiot and a sensualist—little wonder that he is one of the most disagreeable persons in the novel, resenting even the kindness of his foster parents.

In addition to his introduction of Smerdyakov and the boy's background, Dostoevsky also presents the first lengthy, analytical description of Dmitri. And with this Karamazov son, Dostoevsky elaborates upon one of his favorite themes: the contradictory impulses within a personality. Often this idea is referred to as the "Madonna-Sodom" opposition, meaning that radical and diametrically opposed feelings exist at the same time within a person. Dmitri uses this concept to help explain his position, saying, "I can't endure the thought that a man of lofty mind and heart begins with the ideal of the Madonna and ends with the ideal of Sodom. What's still more awful is that a man with the ideal of Sodom in his soul does not renounce the ideal of the Madonna."

Dmitri wallows in his emotional mud and mire but, at the same time, longs to imbue his life with utmost purity. He is especially attracted to purity as represented by the Madonna image but, at the same time, finds himself helplessly trapped in a life of orgies; these he equates with the city of Sodom, destroyed by God because of its corruptness.

He says further that when he sinks "into the vilest degradation," that he always reads Schiller's "Hymn to Joy," and "in the very depths of that degradation I begin a hymn of praise. Let me be accursed. Let me be vile and base, only let me kiss the hem of the veil in which my God is shrouded. Though I may be following the devil, I am Thy son, O Lord, and I love Thee, and I feel the joy without which the world cannot stand."

The poem Dmitri refers to tells of the Goddess Ceres' visit to earth as she looked for her daughter. She found man, instead, "sunk in vilest degradation" and displaying total "loathsomeness." In the chorus of the poem Schiller suggests a remedy: "if man," he says, "wants to purge his soul from vileness" he must "cling forever to his ancient Mother Earth." It is to this poem that Dmitri's soul is attracted; the poem is his credo as he seeks the good and beautiful as a refuge from his periods of degradation. But Dmitri seems damned; there is no ready haven for him. He finds that "beauty is a terrible and awful thing." Beauty, for Dmitri, is especially trying when it is embodied in a woman; it evokes his most saintly emotions and simultaneously arouses his most sensual desires. He cannot reconcile this polar madness; he feels washed with purity and, at the same time, sloshed with torrents of base and vile emotions; his sanity is shielded by only a single thought: he is not totally dishonorable. And it is for this reason, to prove to Alyosha that he is honorable though at times low and base, that he narrates the story of his relations with Katerina Ivanovna.

He tempted her to his apartment when she was desperate for money. He planned to use her poverty to satisfy his own needs; he failed. A dramatic reversal occurred and he gave her the money and made not a single demand upon her body.

Dmitri's confusion is compounded by the fact that he knows that his father has offered Grushenka 3,000 rubles for one night of pleasure. He will not allow this to happen. If ever Grushenka accepts the invitation, for whatever reason, Dmitri tells Alyosha that he is forever doomed because he cannot accept the "leavings" from his father. If she does come to the old man, Dmitri warns his brother, he will be forced to kill their father. In fact, he confides, he hates old Karamazov so much that he is afraid "he will suddenly become so loathsome to me" that he will provoke his own murder. Such statements naturally forewarn us that Dmitri is ripe for murder. He is sensually frustrated, financially troubled, and romantically threatened; all these, coupled with his explosive nature, are ample reasons for us to realize that Dmitri is indeed capable of spilling his father's blood.

Throughout Dmitri's narration and throughout many other scenes of this type, Alyosha functions as a so-called father confessor figure. Dmitri is only one of many characters who will confess to Alyosha. His dress, his priest-like attitude, and his willingness to listen without condemnation make him an ideal person to receive such confidence. But he is much more than a Dostoevskian device for the reader. His personality evokes confession. He has an intense need to listen and learn, and understand mankind, and it is this that matches the other characters' powerful urge to talk, to confess, and to be understood.

Chapters 6-11

Summary

Arriving at the Karamazov house, Alyosha finds his father almost drunk, but still at the table with Ivan. They are listening to old Grigory and Smerdyakov arguing, and it is at this point that we learn more about the bastard Karamazov son. Smerdyakov is rather taciturn, somewhat morose, and naturally resents his position. Strangely, however, he even resents his foster parents. Smerdyakov is an enigma, plagued by jealousy, hatred, and epilepsy. In the household, he works as a cook. Years ago old Fyodor sent him off to Moscow for training and since he returned he has functioned only in that capacity. He is a trustworthy sort, all believe, regardless of his sullenness, for they remember that he once returned 300 rubles to Fyodor which the old man lost while drunk.

Smerdyakov, at present, is arguing with his foster father as Alyosha arrives. He asserts that it is permissible for a man to renounce his faith in God in order to save his life. And, to prove that man cannot function by faith alone, he says that no man has enough faith to tell a mountain to move to the sea. He thinks, therefore, that this is reason enough to realize that man may deny God to save his life and later ask for repentance. Curiously, throughout the argument, he seems particularly anxious to please and impress Ivan.

After Karamazov tires of the argument, he sends the servants away, but the conversation manages to return to the subject of religion and in answer to their father's queries, Ivan insists that there is no God. Further, he says, there is no immortality. Alyosha, of course, maintains that God does exist and that through Him man can gain immortality. Karamazov changes the subject. He talks now of women and begins a long, drunken, and cynical narration, centering upon Alyosha's mother. The attack is depraved. Karamazov delights in mocking his late wife's religious beliefs. He is so vicious, in fact, that Alyosha collapses and succumbs to a seizure exactly like the one that Karamazov described as afflicting Alyosha's mother. Ivan bitterly reminds his drunken father that the woman of whom he has spoken so crudely was also Ivan's mother, and, for a moment, old Karamazov is confused, but recalls then that Ivan and Alyosha did indeed have the same mother. The two are attempting to revive Alyosha as Dmitri dashes into the house.

Karamazov is startled and runs for protection and when he hears Dmitri shout that Grushenka is in the house, the old man grows even more excited and fearful. Dmitri runs frantically through the house trying to discover Grushenka, then returns to the dining room, where old Karamazov begins screaming that Dmitri has been stealing money from him. Dmitri seizes his father, flings him to the floor, and kicks him in the head; then before leaving, he threatens to return and kill the old man, shouting, "Beware, old man, beware of your dreams, because I have my dream too." And he dashes out to continue his search for Grushenka.

After Ivan and Alyosha bandage their father's wounds and put him to bed, Alyosha remains with him for a while, then leaves to go talk with Katerina Ivanovna. He stops in the yard and talks a bit with Ivan and this is the first time that Ivan has been cordial to his brother.

Alyosha arrives at Madame Hohlakov's home and asks for Katerina. The girl is anxious about Dmitri and promises to help save him, although he seems not to want her help; she is positive, though, that his infatuation for Grushenka will pass. Alyosha is greatly surprised to hear Katerina call Grushenka by name and he is even more surprised when he discovers that Grushenka has been hiding behind a screen, listening to their conversation. Katerina explains that Grushenka has just confessed to her that she will soon be reunited with a man whom she has loved for five years. Obviously Katerina is overjoyed at the news and, as she explains the new turn of events to Alyosha, she impulsively kisses and fondles Grushenka, calling her endearing names. She asks Grushenka to affirm what she has just said but Grushenka surprises them all. She becomes capricious and says that she just might change her mind. She also informs Katerina that she does not return the embraces Katerina has bestowed upon her. Katerina fumes. She has humbled herself in gratitude before Grushenka and is furious at the girl's flippancy. She lashes out with stinging, angry insults, but Grushenka merely laughs and walks out, leaving Katerina in hysterics.

Alyosha also leaves the house but on the way out, he is stopped by a maid, who gives him a letter. She tells him that it is from Lise. Alyosha continues his way back to the monastery but is stopped once more, this time by Dmitri. His brother is lighthearted and seems wholly unconcerned about the earlier events of the evening. He listens now to

Alyosha explain what has happened between Katerina and Grushenka
and seems delighted. He laughs at Grushenka's actions and calls her
affectionately his "she-devil." But suddenly his face darkens and he
moans that he is a scoundrel. Nothing, he swears to Alyosha, "can
compare in baseness with the dishonor which I bear now at this very
minute on my breast."

The events of the night have been unnerving and, back at the monastery, Alyosha receives more bad news: Zossima's condition has wors-
ened; he has only a short time to live. Deeply saddened by his family's
sorrows, Alyosha nevertheless decides to remain close to the elder, for
this man is also his father. And having made his decision, he begins
to prepare for bed, then remembers Lise's letter and reads it. It is a love
letter; she says that she loves Alyosha very much and hopes to marry
him when she is old enough. She apologizes sincerely for making fun
of the young priest and implores him to come visit her.

Commentary

Dostoevsky carefully details in this book the special sort of characterization needed for the enigmatic Smerdyakov, the son who will murder Karamazov. We learn, for example, that he "seemed to despise
everybody," including his real father and also his foster father. It is
clear that he could conceivably murder either one, and in cold blood,
and furthermore we learn that in childhood that "he was very fond of
hanging cats," certainly a sadistic and perverse pastime. As a comple-
ment to his psychological ills, he is physically sick; epilepsy overtakes
him on occasion, a disease he inherited from his idiot mother. Of late,
nervous fits have attacked him increasingly and it is one of these attacks
that he later shams as his alibi when his innocence is questioned.

In his argument with Grigory, put forward to impress the intellectual Ivan, Smerdyakov uses the most basic semantic logic to prove his
point. But the argument shows that he is interested in questions similar
to those that disturb Ivan. And it is in this way that Dostoevsky sets up
conflicting emotions within Ivan. Because of their like interests he is
drawn to his half-brother, but at the same time, with a Dostoevskian
duality of emotion, he is repulsed and sees him as a "mean soul."

The vulgarity of old Karamazov is once more emphasized in this
section. This time, in the presence of Alyosha, he crudely ridicules
his son's mother. This is a particularly painful scene because we have
been told that Alyosha remembers his mother with deep love and respect.

The father's attack, then, believably brings on Alyosha's convulsions. Karamazov commits a verbal murder on Alyosha's memories and it is significant, following Alyosha's collapse, that Karamazov does not realize that the same woman gave birth to both Ivan and Alyosha. In other words, the two sons are so different that the old man has completely forgotten that they had the same mother.

In Chapter 9, when Dmitri unleashes an uncontrollable fit of anguish and knocks down first Grigory and later his father, Dostoevsky is tempering our credence in Dmitri's being a potential murderer. Both father and son are victims of powerful emotions and both are passionate sensualists; their antagonism and hatred has, at present, collided over the same woman. It is likely that such viciousness as we witness might result in murder.

Even Alyosha realizes the possibility of parricide within his family when he questions Ivan as to a man's right to assess another man and decide whether or not he is worthy to live. And Ivan too realizes the potential of parricide as it smoulders, for he answers Alyosha that "one reptile will devour the other."

In Chapter 10 we are introduced finally to the beautiful and the paradoxical Katerina Ivanovna. Several times we have heard of this lovely and haughty woman, willing to devote herself to Dmitri in spite of his barbarous forays. Now we see her. She absolutely refuses to accept Dmitri's breaking of their engagement. And the extremity of her resolve is so resolute that she even humbles herself before Grushenka.

As for Grushenka, she turns out to be far more interesting than gossip suggests. She may or may not be waiting for a scoundrel who deserted her five years earlier. And it is his return, incidentally, that precipitates the pivotal action of the novel. Grushenka's mercurial qualities are quite thorough; she is whimsical and mischievous and does seem as though she might be, as Dmitri laughingly tags her, a "she-devil." She is more than a tease, however, and immediately after the murder she realizes that she, in large part, is to blame for keeping both Dmitri and his father in suspense as to what she actually intends for them.

Dmitri's confession of baseness to Alyosha is in reference to his retention of the 1,500 rubles that he saved from the night of the Grushenka orgy; this money he has not yet returned to Katerina. And his keeping it burdens his scheme of values with far greater dishonor than the fact that he spent the other half of the sum. Later it is this anguish of

Dmitri's over the money he did not spend which convinces many people that such a man could not commit a murder.

At the monastery, Alyosha still does not know why Zossima has ordered him to go into the world. "Here was peace. Here was holiness"; one can easily lose one's way in the world, Alyosha realizes, and go astray. It is, though, exactly for these reasons that the elder has asked him to go into the world. Alyosha is the one person who will be able to walk through confusion and darkness and not lose his footing. At this moment, his father, Katerina, Lise, Dmitri, and Grushenka are all waiting to talk with him again; his life's work is among the people of the world who need his quiet example of love and respect.

PART TWO

BOOK IV

Summary

Nearing death, Father Zossima rallies a bit and gathers his friends and disciples around him. He speaks to them of the necessity of loving one another and all men and urges them to remember that each human being shares a responsibility for the sins of all others.

Alyosha leaves the cell, aware of the tense sorrow that hovers over the monastery. All members of the holy community, he is sure, anticipate some sort of miracle, one occurring immediately after the elder's death. There are, in fact, already rumors of Father Zossima's being responsible for a recent miracle. Not quite all, however, share Alyosha's idealization of Zossima. Living in the monastery is another very old monk, Father Ferapont, "antagonistic to Father Zossima and the whole institution of elders." Ferapont believes in a religion based upon severe fasting and upon fear of Satan, a belief totally opposite to the doctrine of love advocated by Father Zossima. Ferapont sees the devil at work in all things and frequently has visions of lurking devils, waiting to ensnare innocent souls. He is admired by only a few people because of such severity, but he does have a coterie of staunch followers.

After Father Zossima has retired to his cell, he calls for Alyosha and reminds the boy that he hopes Alyosha will return to the town in order to fulfill his responsibilities to his father and to his brothers. Alyosha acquiesces.

On his return, Alyosha finds his father alone. The old man insists that he plans to live a long time, but that he needs much money to attract young "wenches" to come to him in his later years, when he has lost much of his vigor. He vehemently proclaims that above all other things, he will remain a sensualist until he is forced to bed down with death.

Alyosha listens, then leaves his father's house. Outside he encounters a group of schoolboys throwing rocks at an outcast young lad, a frail young child about nine years old. Despite his fraility, however, the boy returns the violence and flings back sharp rocks at the squadron of young hoodlums. Then suddenly he breaks and runs. Alyosha dashes after the boy, anxious to discover what lies under such antagonism. But when he catches him the youngster is sullen and defiant. He hits Alyosha with a rock and lunges at him, biting his hand. He escapes once more and leaves Alyosha perplexed as to the meaning of such corrosive bitterness.

Alyosha's next stop is at the home of Madame Hohlakov. There he is surprised to learn that Ivan is also a visitor, upstairs at the moment with Katerina. Dmitri's presence might have been in order, but certainly Ivan's is unexpected to the young Karamazov. He asks for some cloth to bandage his hand and when Madame Hohlakov goes in search of medication, he is immediately set upon by Lise. She implores him to return her letter; it was a bad joke, she says. But Alyosha refuses to part with the letter. He believed its contents, he says, but he cannot return it; he does not have it with him. Alyosha then leaves Lise and goes to talk with Ivan and Katerina.

Katerina repeats to Alyosha what she has just told Ivan — that she will never abandon Dmitri, even if he marries Grushenka. Furthermore, she intends to help and protect him even though he does not appreciate it. Ivan agrees with her, though he admits that in another woman such behavior would be considered thoroughly neurotic. Alyosha can no longer retain himself. He tries to convince them that they love each other; they are only torturing themselves by their theorizings. Ivan admits that he does love Katerina, but says that she needs someone like Dmitri because of her excessive self-esteem. Then he says that he is leaving the next day for Moscow and excuses himself.

After Ivan leaves, Katerina tells Alyosha of a poor captain, a Mr. Snegiryov, who was once brutally beaten by Dmitri while the captain's young son stood by and begged for mercy. She has never forgotten the incident and asks Alyosha to take 200 rubles to the captain as a token of her deep sympathy. Alyosha says that he will do as she asks and leaves.

The captain in question lives in a ramshackle old house with a mentally deranged wife, two daughters (one of whom is a crippled hunchback), and his young son, Ilusha. Coincidentally, Ilusha turns out to be the outcast who earlier bit Alyosha's hand. Before Alyosha can explain why he has come, the boy cries out that the young Karamazov has come to complain about the hand-biting. And it is then that Alyosha understands why the boy attacked him so savagely: he was defending his father's honor against a Karamazov.

The captain takes Alyosha outside and tells him the story of his encounter with Dmitri and how terribly the episode affected his young son. He further emphasizes the family's poverty, and Alyosha — overjoyed that he can relieve the old man's poverty — explains that he has come to give him 200 rubles. The captain is delighted by such unexpected good luck and speaks of the many things he can now do for his sick and hungry family. But suddenly he changes his mind. With a proud gesture, he throws the money to the ground, saying that if he accepts the sum he can never gain his son's love and respect. Alyosha retrieves the money and starts back to Katerina to report his failure.

Commentary

At the end of Book III, Alyosha wonders why Father Zossima has asked him to leave the monastery. Book IV is Dostoevsky's explanation. From chapter to chapter, Alyosha moves among the characters as they grapple with their assorted problems. He fast becomes the living embodiment of the elder's teachings. Each chapter illustrates Alyosha's influences. In Chapter 2 he travels to his father's house and listens to the frustrations that plague the old man. Then he goes to Madame Hohlakov's and tries to pacify young Lise by calmly accepting her hysterical outcries. While there he makes an effort to bring Ivan and Katerina together as lovers. Next, he goes to the cottage of the destitute Captain Snegiryov. Obviously Dostoevsky intends us to see that Alyosha is meant for a life of activity, not for the quiet passivity of the monastery.

The message of Father Zossima is of particular importance in this book. Earlier he has emphasized the value of love and has admonished his adherents to love one another, to love all of God's people. Now he reminds his followers that simply because they have assumed a monastic life does not imply that they are more blessed than other people. In fact, "from the very fact of coming here, each of us has confessed to himself that he is worse than others." He also reminds his listeners that each man is responsible for every other man and "that he is responsible to all men for all and everything, for all human sins, national and individual." This speech alone contains all the reasons for Alyosha's leaving the monastery. A life of seclusion does not test one's strength if he is to be a representative of Zossima's theories. The elder's ideas can be tested only in the midst of busy society.

Father Zossima's ideas concerning the responsibility of one man for another can take on added weight in the conversations that Alyosha has with Ivan. Ivan refuses to take the responsibility for Dmitri's sins and tells Alyosha that he is not his brother's keeper. And later, Zossima's concept of responsibility triggers Alyosha into considering his own responsibility for Karamazov's murder.

At the end of Zossima's talk, rumors are spread of a forthcoming miracle, one that will coincide with the elder's death. Alyosha is intrigued by the rumors, especially since he believes Zossima to be saintlike, but he is sorely tested when his beloved elder's body rapidly decomposes.

As Alyosha begins his journey through the complex world of society, he goes first to his father's house and listens to all kinds of vulgar and disgusting stories. His father tells him that he will need much money in later years to tempt young "wenches" to sleep with him and suggests that Ivan is trying to marry Katerina so that Dmitri will have to marry Grushenka; thus old Karamazov will be prevented from remarrying and leaving his fortune to a new wife—in other words—to Grushenka. All these wild accusations color more darkly Dostoevsky's portrait of Karamazov as a repulsive and bestial type. Throughout the confession, Alyosha is able to retain his peaceful mein and never compromises his inner nature of dignity and love.

In the scene with young Ilusha, Alyosha still remains the perfectly self-contained individual. He does not even use any violence when Ilusha bites him so viciously. It is a bitter entrance into the world— stoned and bitten only because one is a Karamazov; none of this, of course, would have happened if Alyosha had remained in seclusion at the monastery.

But Alyosha has made his choice according to Zossima's wishes and according to the dictates of the elder who told him that he must marry and become one with the world. He, therefore, tells the young invalid Lise that when she comes of age they will marry.

As for another marriage — one between Ivan and Katerina — the solution is not quite so simple. They are apparently in love with each other, but both are so arrogant that they cannot come to an understanding. Part of the difficulty lies in Katerina's fantastic personality. She feels the need to suffer or to be humiliated by Dmitri and her statement that she will never abandon Dmitri, even if he marries Grushenka indicates the fanatical degree to which she plans to carry her suffering and martyrdom. Ivan well sums up her peculiar nature when he says that she needs Dmitri "so as to contemplate continually your heroic fidelity and to reproach him for infidelity."

For the present, then, Katerina's declaration results in an impasse; her views toward the two brothers will not be resolved until the trial and even then real objectivity will be impossible. Nevertheless, it is true that she feels the need to be humiliated by Dmitri. Proof of this lies in her deep sympathy with Captain Snegiryov, a man who has been humiliated by Dmitri. She asks Alyosha to take him 200 rubles "as a token of sympathy," but her sympathy is far greater than token value.

Alyosha fast becomes involved in social intrigues. But one should be aware that there is no rancor or bitterness in his new role. Alyosha has no resentment, even following the Ilusha incident. Quite the contrary, he has great compassion for a young boy who will try and defend his father's honor. Book IV, then places the neophyte Alyosha in a variety of new situations and the boy's skill in dealing with them suggests the future potential that Father Zossima sensed in him. Looking ahead, however, one might note that success is not total. Further along, it will become apparent that Alyosha often fails with adults. But it is with children that he most succeeds; with the younger generation his qualities of quiet love and devotion find the most fertile sympathy. This, of course, is part of Dostoevsky's vision — children represent the future of all hope and salvation and in this novel Alyosha entrusts Zossima's ideal of love and honor to the new generation.

BOOK V

Chapters 1-4

Summary

When Alyosha returns to Madame Hohlakov's to report his failure with the captain, he learns that Katerina has developed a fever following her hysterical outburst and is now upstairs, unconscious. To Lise, Alyosha explains the nature of his mission and his failure, and analyzes the captain's character for her. As he talks, Lise becomes very impressed with such deep insight and such warmth and love of humanity. She confesses that she indeed meant what she wrote in the letter. The revelation is startling and she and Alyosha discuss their feelings for each other and begin to make plans for marriage. For his part, Alyosha admits that he has told a white lie concerning the letter. He did not return it, not because he did not have it, but because he valued it too much.

Meanwhile, Madame Hohlakov, who has eavesdropped on the conversation, stops Alyosha as he is leaving and expresses deep disapproval of the match. Alyosha assures her that the marriage is yet far in the future, that Lise is much too young to presently marry.

Alyosha then, puzzling over Dmitri's actions of the previous night, decides to try and find his brother. It is more important, he believes, to "have saved something" of Dmitri's honor than to flee back to the monastery. The summerhouse seems a likely place to find his brother; this is where he often watches for Grushenka and dreams of her. As Alyosha waits, he overhears Smerdyakov singing and playing the guitar for the housekeeper's daughter. Alyosha interrupts, with apologies, and asks Smerdyakov if he has seen Dmitri. The cook is able to help Alyosha and says that Ivan has made an appointment to meet Dmitri at the Metropolis restaurant. Alyosha rushes there but Dmitri is not to be found. Instead, Ivan is dining alone. Ivan beckons to his brother and Alyosha accepts his brother's invitation to talk. Ivan admits, first off, that he is anxious to know Alyosha better; he has come to respect and admire the boy. Ivan also admits that he has an intense longing for life even though he constantly encounters only disorder and injustice. Alyosha, however, is more concerned about Dmitri and what will happen to him and what will happen to Fyodor if Ivan leaves the family. To this, Ivan insists that he is absolutely not his brother's keeper, nor his father's keeper, and confesses finally that he is dining at the restaurant for only one reason: he cannot bear the presence of his loathsome father.

That settled, Ivan begins to tell Alyosha of his views on "the existence of God and immortality." He says that he does not reject God but, on the other hand, he cannot accept Him. If God does exist and if he indeed created the world, the human mind should be able to fathom the deed and understand the purpose of creation. Ivan cannot and therefore rejects the world God created. If, he adds, this means that he must reject God, then that is another problem. Alyosha queries more closely, asking Ivan to be more specific as to why he cannot accept the world. Ivan answers by saying that he can love man at a distance but that he is unable to love his next door neighbor. For him "Christ-like love for men is a miracle impossible on earth." That which makes it especially difficult to accept the world, as it is, is the vast suffering and brutality in the world. If God exists, says Ivan, how can this horror be accounted for? He singles out the suffering of children as prime evidence of the world's indifferent cruelty. Children have had no time to sin, but they suffer. Why? Certainly not because of sin — supposedly the cause of suffering. He then recites several horrible examples of atrocities inflicted upon children by other human beings. Because such injustice is allowed to happen, Ivan simply cannot accept the mythical "harmony of God," or accept a universe where one who is tortured embraces his torturer. Such "harmony," says Ivan, "is not worth the tears of one tortured child." He concludes that if truth must be bought at the price of the suffering of children, then such truth is not worth the price. He tells Alyosha: "It's not God that I don't accept, Alyosha, only I most respectfully return Him the ticket."

Alyosha is horrified and tells Ivan that these thoughts constitute rebellion. Ivan offers Alyosha a further example: suppose, he says, one could create a perfect world for man but it could only survive by torturing to death "one tiny creature." Would Alyosha be the architect of such a world? As an answer, Ivan is reminded that there is One who can forgive everything "because He gave His innocent blood for all and everything." Ivan assures his brother that he has not forgotten "the One without sin," and recites a prose poem which he wrote several years ago. He calls his poem "The Grand Inquisitor."

Commentary

As Alyosha tells Lise of his encounter with the captain, we see that he, like Zossima, has a deeply penetrating mind and understands the inner workings of those whom he is trying to help. It is this understanding of human nature that proves Alyosha much more than a simple person of simple faith.

Zossima, remember, has commanded Alyosha to marry and, because of the elder, Alyosha has chosen Lise; no one, he believes, will make him a better wife. But for all of Zossima's influence, he is not a puppet-master. Alyosha is objective about the wisdom of his mentor's teachings and although he knows that Zossima is dying, he feels that it is a higher duty to find Dmitri than go to the elder's deathbed. Thus

Alyosha matures into a man of worldly responsibility and makes other men much more than only of spiritual concern.

In Chapter 3, Dostoevsky makes clear the earlier ambiguities of Ivan's character. Previously, the brother has maintained a distance from Alyosha because he has been evaluating him to see if he is merely an empty-minded religious fanatic. Now, however, Ivan has learned to respect and admire Alyosha because "you do stand firm and I like people who are firm like that, whatever it is that they stand by." Ivan is now ready to thoroughly discuss his beliefs with his brother. In addition, Ivan also feels that his impending departure makes it imperative to explain himself to Alyosha. But if he is concerned with Alyosha, he is certainly not concerned for Dmitri; he absolutely refuses to be either his brother's keeper or the "keeper" of Fyodor. He is quite adamant concerning this and his vehemence is easily recalled when the idea of Fyodor's being vulnerable for murder is discussed.

Preluding his views on religion, Ivan announces that he has a strong desire to live. He loves life even though he finds it illogical. Such an acknowledgement of a love of living is important because Ivan, with a philosophy seemingly nihilistic, might too easily be categorized as a suicidal cynic. Ivan is morally much stronger and is deeply committed to the business of living.

Both brothers, Ivan and Alyosha, agree that "for real Russians the questions of God's existence and of immortality...come first and foremost and so they should." And, in its largest context, this is the subject of the novel. These ideas are central not just to the characters, but to an understanding of Dostoevsky's entire point of view.

Ivan surprises Alyosha by announcing "perhaps I too accept God," reminding his brother of the saying, "If God did not exist, it would be necessary to invent Him," because for Ivan the astonishing factor of Christianity is that man is basically such a "savage, vicious beast," that it is illogical that he could conceive of an idea so noble and magnificent as "God." Ivan is, of course, leading into his views about the baseness of most humans and the difficulty of believing man sufficiently noble to conceive of something so totally transcending his own vicious nature.

Most of all, Ivan desires a world in which his human intellect can fully comprehend the logic and purpose of life. He uses the analogy of two parallel lines which, according to Euclid, can never meet. Ivan's mind can comprehend this concept because he has a "Euclidian earthly mind." But if someone tells him that two parallel lines might meet somewhere in infinity and even if he sees it himself, he still cannot accept the theory. Therefore, even though he is willing to accept God, His Wisdom, and His purpose, he cannot accept "this world of God's . . . it's the world created by Him that I don't and can't accept."

To explain further why he does not accept the world, Ivan examines the brutality found in the world, saying that he cannot love his neighbor. It is easy to love man in the abstract sense, certainly, but when one looks into the face of a man, it is impossible to love him. For Christ, to love men was easy because He was God; but for ordinary men to love one's neighbor — the idea is ridiculously impossible. Later Ivan will elaborate upon this in his poem "The Grand Inquisitor."

Ivan uses the suffering of innocent children as his principal grounds for the world's unacceptability. The idea of the suffering innocent, of course, has plagued philosophers since time's beginning; it is the subject of such great works as the Book of Job. But Ivan does not concern himself with the sufferings of adults. For them, a philosophical justification is possible: the adult has sinned and his suffering is a punishment for his sins. Children, however, have not yet sinned and therefore Ivan cannot understand a world created by God which justifies their suffering. And regardless of whether one agrees or disagrees with Ivan, one must recognize the logic at work in this system of thinking. Life, for Ivan, must be rational — it must especially be rational if one is to appreciate God's wonder and love Him as one should.

So well has Ivan considered his philosophy that he is even amused by the term "bestial cruelty," for this, he believes, is an insult to beasts. An animal kills only for food and kills rapidly, but man kills slowly, deliberately, and often only for the sadistic pleasure of watching his victim suffer.

As Ivan speaks, he is quite aware that he is causing Alyosha to suffer; he knows well of Alyosha's fondness for children. But, although he is not his "brother's keeper," he is far from heartless and, for him, children are revered. He can find no logic that justifies their suffering. And he asks Alyosha what would be the basis of an eternal harmony if a victim would "rise up and embrace his murderer." If this higher harmony would, even in part, be based upon such suffering, then Ivan must renounce it. Truth is not worth such a price. In reference to the story of the general who had his dogs kill a peasant boy, Ivan states, "I don't want the mother to embrace the oppressor who threw her son to the dogs! She dare not forgive him! Let her forgive him for herself, if she will, let her forgive the torturer for the immeasurable suffering of her mother's heart. But the sufferings of her tortured child she has no right to forgive; she dare not forgive the torturer, even if the child were to forgive him!" Ivan rejects such monstrous injustice; he would rather remain with his "unavenged suffering and unsatisfied indignation."

When Alyosha tells Ivan that his view is that of rebellion, Ivan presents Alyosha with the following hypothesis: "Imagine you are creating a fabric of human destiny with the object of making men happy in the end, giving them peace and rest at last, but that it was essential and inevitable to torture to death only one tiny creature... to found that edifice on its unavenged tears, would you consent to be the architect on those conditions?" This analogy of Ivan's offers the same view as that expressed throughout the chapter — that a world created for men should not be founded on innocent suffering. As a humanist, Ivan cannot accept happiness or eternal harmony at the expense of any "unexpiated blood."

Alyosha reminds Ivan that he has forgotten the one Being Who "gave His innocent blood for all" and that it is because of Alyosha's objection that Ivan is provoked to narrate his prose poem, "The Grand Inquisitor."

Chapter 5

Summary

During the sixteenth century in Spain, at the height of the Inquisition, someone resembling Christ appears unannounced in the streets. The people recognize Him immediately and begin to flock about Him. But, as He is healing several of the sick and lame, an old cardinal also recognizes Him and orders the guards to arrest Him. Once again Christ is abducted.

That night, He receives a visitor. The Grand Inquisitor enters the darkened cell and begins a severe reprimand of Christ for appearing again and hindering the work of the church. The Grand Inquisitor explains to Christ that, because of His rejection of the three temptations, He placed an intolerable burden of freedom upon man. The church, however, is now correcting His errors and aiding man by removing their awful burden of freedom. He explains that Christ erred when He expected man to voluntarily choose to follow Him. The basic nature of man, says the Inquisitor, does not allow him to reject either earthly bread or security or happiness in exchange for something so indefinite as what Christ expects.

If Christ had accepted the proffered bread, man would have been given security instead of a freedom of choice and if Christ had performed a miracle and had cast himself down from the pinnacle, man would have been given something miraculous to worship. The nature of man, insists the Inquisitor, is to seek the miraculous. Finally, Christ should have accepted the power offered Him by the devil. Because He did not, the church has now had to assume such power for the benefit of man. And since Christ's death, the church has been forced to correct the errors made by Him. Now, at last mankind willingly submits its freedom to the church in exchange for happiness and security. This balance, says the Inquisitor, must not be upset.

At the end of the monolog, the Grand Inquisitor admits that of necessity he is on the side of the devil, but the challenge that Christ placed on mankind allows only a few strong people to be saved; the rest must be sacrificed to these strong. The Grand Inquisitor's scheme, at least, provides an earthly happiness for the mass of mankind even though it will not lead to eternal salvation. On the other hand, Christ's method would not have saved these same weak and puny men either.

When he finishes, the Grand Inquisitor looks at Christ. He has remained silent the entire time. Now He approaches the old churchman and kisses him on his dry, withered lips. The Grand Inquisitor frees Him suddenly, saying that He is never to come again.

Ivan finishes his story and wonders now if Alyosha will reject him or will try to accept him as a brother. As an answer, Alyosha leans forward and kisses his brother. "You are plagarizing my poem," Ivan cries in delight. The brothers leave the restaurant together, but they then part, each going his separate way.

Commentary

In the chapter preceding "The Grand Inquisitor," Ivan has struggled with the problem of suffering humanity and the injustice of this world. Now he turns to one of the major philosophical questions—one which has worried the Western world for centuries: the awesome burden placed upon man by his having complete freedom instead of church-directed happiness and security.

Dostoevsky achieves his dramatic impact in this chapter by having the two antagonists embody the two ideas in question—the Grand Inquisitor pleading for security and happiness for man; Christ offering complete freedom. Furthermore, the advocate for freedom—the reincarnate Christ—remains completely silent throughout the Inquisitor's monolog; his opponent does all the talking. Yet the old Inquisitor is no mere egotist. His character is one that evokes our respect. We consider his position in the church, his intellect, his certainty, and above all, his professed love for mankind. All this he does in spite of the fact that, as he finally admits, he has aligned himself with Satan.

The complexity of the Grand Inquisitor increases when we realize that he, like his divine opponent, has been in the wilderness and could have stood among the elect, but deliberately chose to take his stand with the weak and puny mass of mankind. And just as Ivan, in the preceding chapter, declared that even if God could justify innocent suffering, he would refuse to accept the explanation, so the Grand Inquisitor also affirms this stand. The two—Ivan and the Grand Inquisitor—are in close accord and much of the Grand Inquisitor is also seen in Ivan's questioning and perplexity. The two are also kissed by their opponents, Christ and Alyosha.

In the tale, when Christ reappears, the Grand Inquisitor has begun to build a world upon the concepts of authority, miracle, and mystery. And, as a cardinal, he speaks and commands with unquestionable authority. When he sees Christ performing miracles among the people, he has merely to hold out his finger and bid the guards take Him. The townspeople are cowed by him; they tremblingly obey him.

The church-conceived way to salvation and its strong-arm authority are targets for Dostoevsky and, through Ivan, he builds up a case of condemnation against the Roman Catholic church. The Grand Inquisitor, for example, visiting Christ in the night says to Him, "Thou hast no right to add anything to what Thou hadst said of old." That is, Christ has said all that was necessary. Since then the church has taken over with its great authority and established what should—and what should not—be believed. The church, not Christ, is the supreme authority in matters of faith and conduct. "Why hast Thou come to hinder us," he asks Christ and, to make sure that He does not overthrow the centuries of authority of the church, he says that he will "condemn Thee and burn Thee at the stake as the worst of heretics."

The argument between the Grand Inquisitor and Christ is made especially effective because Dostoevsky arranges their meeting on ancient terms: Christ is once again the prisoner, the accused, yet He does not defend Himself. Ironically, it is the executioner who must defend himself. The prisoner never utters a word. But it is wrong to see them as hero and villain. Both men—one silently, the other verbosely —argue for the best way in which man can achieve happiness. Both have humanistic motives and love for the mass of mankind. Their end result —happiness for man—is identical; only by definition and method do the men vary.

The Grand Inquisitor criticizes Christ for wishing to set man free, asking "Thou hast seen these 'free' men?" For fifteen centuries the problem of freedom has weighed heavily on both the church and mankind but now, says the Inquisitor, the church has "vanquished freedom and has done so to make men happy." His pity for the weakness of man has made him realize that man cannot handle such a burdensome problem as freedom and, to prove this point, he reminds Christ of the temptations He was tested by.

The source for the Grand Inquisitor's view is found in St. Luke, 4:1-13—

And Jesus being full of the Holy Ghost returned from Jordan, and was led by the Spirit into the wilderness,

Being forty days tempted of the devil. And in those days he did eat nothing: and when they were ended, he afterward hungered.

And the devil said unto him, If thou be the Son of God, command this stone that it be made bread.

And Jesus answered him, saying, It is written, That man shall not live by bread alone, but by every word of God.

And the devil, taking him up into a high mountain, showed unto him all the kingdoms of the world in a moment of time.

And the devil said unto him, All this power will I give thee, and the glory of them: for that is delivered unto me; and to whomsoever I will, I give it.

If thou therefore wilt worship me, all shall be thine.

And Jesus answered and said unto him, Get thee behind me, Satan: for it is written, Thou shalt worship the Lord thy God, and him only shalt thou serve.

And he brought him to Jerusalem, and set him on a pinnacle of the temple, and said unto him, If thou be the Son of God, cast thyself down from hence:

For it is written, He shall give his angels charge over thee, to keep thee:

And in *their* hands they shall bear thee up, lest at any time thou dash thy foot against a stone.

And Jesus answering said unto him, It is said, Thou shalt not tempt the Lord thy God.

And when the devil had ended all the temptation, he departed from him for a season.

An important question evoked by this passage is whether or not Christ was refusing the temptations — security through bread, authority, and miracle — for Himself alone, or whether by refusing He was doing so for all mankind and placing a burden too tremendous upon such a frail creature as man. If Christ refused solely for Himself, His refusal does not carry such heavy implications because He was divine and could easily afford to resist such temptations. But if He was refusing for all mankind, then it follows that He expects man to believe in something intangible even while He does not have enough to eat.

To complicate the matter, the Grand Inquisitor places his questions in the terms of being asked by "the wise and dread spirit," who offers Christ three things. Christ is clearly the rejector, but not for Himself alone — for all mankind. And when the Grand Inquisitor states, "The statement of those three questions was itself the miracle," he means that Satan is so wording his questions that the future fate of all mankind will be determined. He asks Christ to "Judge Thyself who was right — Thou or he who questioned Thee."

The first question is viewed in terms of freedom versus security. By refusing the bread, Christ is insisting that man must have freedom to choose to follow Him without being lulled into a sense of security by being provided with bread. If bread is provided, then man loses his freedom to choose Christ voluntarily. "Thou wouldst not deprive men of freedom and didst reject the offer, thinking what is that freedom worth, if obedience is bought with bread." The Grand Inquisitor feels that what Christ wants for man is impossible. "Nothing," he says, "has ever been more insupportable for a man and a human society than freedom." By denying bread or security for man and by giving man in its stead the freedom to follow Him of his own volition, Christ failed to understand the human nature of men who are "weak, vicious, worthless, and rebellious." To promise the bread of heaven to a man starving for earthly bread and to expect him to choose the former of his own volition, puts an insufferable weight upon mankind who must, by nature, reject Christ in favor of whoever offers earthly bread. The Grand Inquisitor cries, "Feed men and then ask of them virtue."

Instead of freeing all mankind, Christ (charges the Grand Inquisitor) succeeded only in freeing the strong. The tens of thousands who have the strength to voluntarily accept heavenly bread follow Him but what, asks the Inquisitor, is to become of the tens of millions who are too weak to accept, responsibly, the dreadful freedom of choice? Are the weak to be condemned for the sake of the elect who have the strength to follow after the heavenly bread?

The Grand Inquisitor says that he has corrected Christ's errors. He has done so because he loves the weak who hunger after earthly bread. Man is now fed by the church and, in return, has willingly relinquished his former freedom for security. "Man seeks to worship what is established beyond dispute" so that he will not have to face the dreadful "freedom of choice." If Christ had only chosen the bread, He then would "have satisfied the universal and ever-lasting craving for humanity—to find someone to worship." Christ erred in rejecting earthly bread for the sake of freedom. "Instead of taking men's freedom from them, Thou didst make it greater than ever! Didst Thou forget that man prefers peace and even death to freedom of choice in the knowledge of good and evil?"

Also, by His rejection of earthly bread, Christ forced man to choose between solid security as opposed to something that is "exceptional, vague, and enigmatic. Thou didst choose what was utterly beyond the strength of men. Instead of taking possession of man's freedom, Thou didst increase it and burdened the spiritual kingdom of mankind with its suffering forever." Now each individual man must decide for himself "what is good and what is evil, having only Thy Image before him." Had Christ truly loved mankind, He should have had more compassion and should have understood man's inherent weaknesses.

The Grand Inquisitor explains then that he (the church) has compassion and understanding for man and has given him "miracle, mystery, and authority." The church tells men what to believe and what to choose and thereby relieves him of choosing for himself. At last man has a sense of security which Christ denied him.

By miracle, the Grand Inquisitor explains that when Christ rejected the second temptation—the refusal to cast Himself down—he was rejecting one of the essential characteristics man expects from religion —the truly miraculous. Of course, Christ, as divine, could reject the miraculous, but He should have understood that the nature of man desires a miracle. "But Thou didst not know that when man rejects miracles he rejects God also; for man seeks not so much God as the miraculous. And as man cannot bear to be without the miraculous, he will create new miracles of his own for himself and will worship deeds of sorcery and witchcraft." In other words, man's basic nature is to seek that which transcends human existence; he worships that which is superhuman, that which has a sense of the miraculous.

"We are not working with Thee," the Inquisitor says, "but with *him*—that is our mystery. It's long—eight centuries—since we have been on *his* side and not on Thine. Just eight centuries ago, we took from him what Thou didst reject with scorn, that last gift he offered Thee, showing Thee all the kingdoms of the earth. We took from him Rome and the sword of Caesar."

The church has taken the kingdom of earth—that which Christ rejected. Here the church has established its plan for the universal happiness of man. "Freedom, free thought, and science" will create such insoluble riddles and chaotic disunity that soon, all men will gladly surrender their freedom, saying "You alone possess His mystery...save us from ourselves."

The future world of happiness will be based on a totalitarian state, organized on the principle of total obedience and submission and "they will submit to us gladly and cheerfully...because it will save them from the great anxiety and terrible agony they endure at present in making a free decision for themselves." The church will even allow certain people to sin so long as they are obedient and submissive. Man's happiness will be the happiness of children who have no responsibilities and no choices; all questions will be answered by the church. The only person unhappy will be, ironically, those few who will "guard the mystery." That is, only the members of the church who understand the above concepts will suffer because they will be the "sufferers who have taken upon themselves the curse of the knowledge of good and evil."

Like Ivan, the Grand Inquisitor is unwilling to become one of the few elect when it means that "millions of creatures have been created as a mockery." Only a few people in the world can prize or understand the freedom given them by Christ; these are the strong and the powerful. Out of pity for all mankind, the Grand Inquisitor, who could have been on the side of the elect, repudiates the system that would doom millions of the weak. Such a system is unjust and thus he chooses to accept a system designed for the multitudes of the weak rather than for the few of the strong.

At one point, the Grand Inquisitor says that he must burn Christ so that "man will not have to be plagued with that horrible burden of inner freedom." He is a martyr in a special sense because he reserves the privilege of suffering for the few strong people; in this way, the mass of mankind will not have to undergo the terrible suffering associated with absolute freedom. Christ consequently has no right to interfere in the church's organized happiness; He must be punished as an enemy of the people.

At the end of the discussion, Christ responds to the Grand Inquisitor by giving him a kiss on his withered lips. This paradoxical ending undercuts the soliloquy, leaving us to wonder what is right. The reader, however, should remember that Dostoevsky has created two opposite poles of response; man is seldom faced with such clear-cut opposition.

When Alyosha re-enacts the poem and kisses Ivan, it is partly because he recognizes that a man cannot come to such opinions as he has just heard unless he has given them considerable thought; they are obviously the most important questions of mankind. Furthermore, Ivan, like Alyosha, does have a deep love for humanity, a quality that makes anyone worthy of redemption.

Chapters 6-7

Summary

Ivan leaves Alyosha and feels greatly depressed. He cannot understand his depression until he realizes that perhaps it is because of his deep dread of meeting Smerdyakov. He does, however, go home, but seeing the cook sitting in the yard, hopes to pass him without speaking. Strangely, however, he cannot and finds himself greeting his half-brother with great cordiality.

Smerdyakov confesses to Ivan that he too is troubled because of the rivalry between Fyodor and Dmitri for Grushenka. He also fears that the strain of worry might bring on an epileptic seizure. Furthermore, he says, he knows that Dmitri has learned the secret signals that Grushenka is to use if ever she decides to come to Fyodor. If such a meeting occurs, the results could well be tragic: both Grigory and Marfa are ill and Smerdyakov fears that he is ripe for a seizure, and Fyodor will be left alone to face Dmitri's wrath. Ivan wonders why Smerdyakov told Dmitri the secret signals and suggests that perhaps Smerdyakov has arranged matters so that Dmitri will have access to old Fyodor as soon as Ivan leaves for Moscow. Ivan, however, cannot be a watchdog for Karamazov, so resolves to leave the next day for Moscow as planned. Smerdyakov insists that he not go to Moscow, however, that he go to a nearer town, but Ivan is firm and goes to bed without further discussion. The talk has left him exhausted, however, and he finds that he cannot sleep.

Next day, Fyodor pleads with Ivan not to go to Moscow, but to a town close by to sell a copse of wood for the old man. Ivan finally agrees and, as he is leaving, he admits to Smerdyakov that he is not going to Moscow. The servant whispers mysteriously that "it's always worth while speaking to a clever man." Ivan is puzzled.

A few hours later, Smerdyakov falls down the cellar steps and an attack of epilepsy seizes him. He is put to bed and, as predicted, Fyodor is alone. He locks all the doors and windows, then begins his wait for Grushenka. He is certain that she will come to him tonight.

Commentary

Leaving Alyosha, Ivan feels morose and dejected, emotions probably related to the guilt that he feels by associating with Smerdyakov. For even though Ivan does not realize it, he is subconsciously beginning to feel a certain duplicity in his relationships with the servant; the last two chapters, in particular, show how certain actions on Ivan's part implicate him in the murder of old Fyodor.

This fact is also important: Ivan feels a distinct loathing for Smerdyakov. He has entered into many philosophical discussions with him and we learn that they have discussed such questions as how there "could have been light on the first day when the sun, moon, and stars were only created on the fourth day." Smerdyakov, in turn, has discussed things that would impress Fyodor, hoping to make an impression on him and contradict old Grigory. He has, we discover, however, taken most of his ideas from Ivan. Even the idea of the murder came from Ivan.

When Ivan meets the cook, he has planned to say to him, "Get away, miserable idiot. What have I to do with you," but instead he says,

"Is my father still asleep?" This reversal suggests that Ivan is repulsed by this creature but is, at the same time, drawn to him. And, by the same analogy, Ivan is repulsed by the idea that his father will be murdered, but seems also to acquiesce in readying the scene for the hypothetical murder.

In these last chapters one can easily see how completely Smerdyakov has planned the homicide. We hear, first of all, that Dmitri has heard of the secret signals by which Grushenka is to come to the old man. There could, of course, be no reason for Smerdyakov to tell Dmitri about these signals except to lay suspicion on Dmitri when it is known that he was aware of such signals; furthermore, Ivan's ready acceptance of Smerdyakov's explanation indicates that Ivan is also anxious to accept such an alibi. Second, Smerdyakov announces that he feels that he will have an epileptic seizure on the following day — the day that Ivan will be absent from the house. Third, Smerdyakov announces that old Grigory will be doped with some strong medicine which Marfa gives him and always saves a bit of for herself; soon both will be in a heavy sleep. Consequently, Smerdyakov has conceived a perfect setting for murder; he has even created perfect alibis. As he announces later to Ivan — everything had to go just as he planned it; otherwise, the murder could never have been accomplished. Ivan even recognized this when he said earlier, "But aren't you trying to arrange it so?" and tried to remove himself from direct responsibility. But ultimately Ivan must take his share in the moral guilt for his father's death.

At the end of Book V most of the machinery is arranged for the murder. Smerdyakov pretends to have his seizure, old Grigory is laid up with illness, Marfa prepares the medicine for them both, and Fyodor anxiously awaits Grushenka.

BOOK VI

Summary

Father Zossima is propped in bed, surrounded by his friends and followers when Alyosha returns to the monastery. The elder is weak but is still quite alert and anxious to talk with his audience. He greets Alyosha affectionately and asks about Dmitri; he says that the bow made to him was an acknowledgment of the intense suffering he foresees for the boy. Alyosha, however, he says, has quite a different future and again he counsels the young monk to return to the world to look after his brothers. In this way, he says, Alyosha will learn to love all of life, to bless life, and to teach those who suffer to love and bless life.

These pleas to Alyosha are Father Zossima's last requests. Now he tells all assembled the reasons why Alyosha is so very special to him. Once, the elder says, he had an older brother who influenced him tremendously. Alyosha bears a particularly strong resemblance to that brother—physically and spiritually. Then Zossima begins to reminisce.

He was born to a noble family of only moderate means. His father died when he was only two years old and he was reared with his mother and the brother he spoke of. The brother, eight years older than Zossima, came under the influence of a freethinker and was soon a source of sorrow to the mother. He ridiculed her religious observances and her devout beliefs. Then, at seventeen, he contracted consumption and the family was advised that he had but a few months to live.

During the months he waited for death, a tremendous spiritual conversion took place in the boy. He became extremely pious and spoke continuously about the need to love all of God's creatures, even the little birds in the garden. He asked the servants to feel that they were his equal and often said that he wished he could be a servant to the servants.

Besides his brother, Zossima says that there has been another influence on him: the Bible. This book, he says, is a testament of the extent of God's love for all men. Zossima mourns for those who cannot find the vast love that he finds contained in the Bible.

But Zossima's affection for the Bible has not been lifelong. As a youth, he was sent to a military academy in St. Petersburg and soon neglected both the Bible and his religious training. After graduation, he led the carefree life that a typical young officer might. He courted a beautiful lady whom, he was sure, returned his affections, but while he was absent she married someone else. Zossima was insulted and immediately challenged her husband to a duel. But, waking on the morning of the duel, he looked out and saw a fresh, clean beauty on all of God's world and he remembered his dying brother's exhortation: love all of God's creatures. He leaped from his bed, apologized to a servant whom he had beaten the night before and made plans for his duel. He would allow his opponent to take the first shot; afterward, Zossima would drop his pistols and beg the man's forgiveness. This he did. But the officers accompanying Zossima were shocked by the strange behavior. They questioned him and were even more surprised at the explanation: he had, he said, decided to resign his military commission and enter a monastery.

Zossima fast became the talk of the town and one night a mysterious stranger visited him. He begged to hear the motives that prompted Zossima's actions. Zossima talked at length to the man and for many nights afterward. Then, after hearing the whole of Zossima's story, the man made a confession of his own: years ago he killed a woman out of passion and someone else was blamed for the deed. The man in question, however, died before he was tried. Now the perpetrator of the deed has wife and children and has become one of the most respected philanthropists in the community. But, he moans to Zossima, he has never found happiness for himself. In spite of an apparently successful life, he has always needed to confess. This, in fact, he finally did, and in public, but no one believed him; they merely thought that he was temporarily deranged. Not long after his confession to Zossima, the man falls ill. The elder visits him and is thanked greatly for his guidance. Zossima, until now, has never revealed the man's secret.

The elder pauses and begins to speak to Alyosha of what it has meant to be a monk. Zossima feels that the Russian monk is, of all persons, closest to the Russian folk and that ultimately the salvation of Russia will come through these common people who, he feels sure, will always remain orthodox in their belief. He also talks of the equality of all people and hopes that everyone can someday be truly meek and can accept a servant as an equal and, in turn, function as a servant to others.

True equality, he says, is found only in the "spiritual dignity of man." As an example, he tells of an old servant's giving him a sum of money for the monastery. This, the elder reveals, is the ideal reversal in action; a master-servant relationship exists no longer.

Zossima admonishes his listeners to love all of God's creatures and to take on the responsibility of all men's sins. He explains that often God expects many things that we cannot understand with human logic. Man, for example, should not judge his fellow men — even criminals — says Zossima; man must pray for those who are outside the church, for there does not exist a material hell. There is only a spiritual hell, he says. He then collapses to the floor and reaches out as though to embrace the earth. Joyfully he gives up his soul to God.

Commentary

The final views of Father Zossima are presented in this book and, because of their positive quality, Dostoevsky inserts them next to the questioning disbeliefs of Ivan Karamazov. They act somewhat like a counterbalance to the many ideas presented in Book V.

Unlike Ivan, Zossima is didactic — the most didactic character in the novel, perhaps in all of Dostoevsky's writings. His ideas are too abstract to be presented as Ivan's were; his ideas are too profound to be presented in any other way than by simple exhortation.

Parts of Zossima's philosophy have, of course, been discussed in earlier books but here almost all of his tenets are gathered together and presented either by examples from his own life or through exhortations and miniature sermons. In one sense, Zossima is an extension of earlier Dostoevskian characters but, because of his personal history, he is much more than a mere abstraction of the author's ideas. Surprisingly, Father Zossima is a rather robust character, one who undergoes many and diverse experiences before dedicating his life to the monastery. There are reasons for his convictions; he is no conventional saint.

Concerning the amount of background material that Zossima gives, it is most important that we see him against such relief. If the elder's theories are to be accepted as valid, we cannot view him as an isolated or even as a repressed person who turns to religion in order to escape the world's rejection. Zossima was not an introvert; his youth was wild and reckless, filled with "drunkenness, debauchery, and devilry." He was popular with his fellow officers and with people in general. His conversion and his subsequent religious dedication, therefore, are grounded in motivated reality.

The account of the duel and Zossima's actions show him to be a person of physical courage as well as of moral courage. It is significant that the conversion was brought about by his remembering some of his dead brother's ideas about loving life and respecting all things in this world. From this time onward, these ideas become more and more central to Zossima's final philosophy of life.

Concerning suffering, Zossima's explanation of why he bowed down to Dmitri has its roots deep in Dostoevskian philosophy. In *Crime and Punishment,* for example, the protagonist bows down before a prostitute because he sees in her "the suffering of all humanity." Suffering, Dostoevsky felt, was the genesis of retribution. Only through great suffering can a man be purified of his sins and it is this process that Zossima sees within Dmitri.

In speaking of his love for the Bible, Zossima says that the book's basic lesson is this: one must realize the vast love that God has for mankind. At first, admittedly, such a realization is not easy. It is difficult to accept God giving his beloved Job to the devil for no other reason than to boast to his opponent. But the value of the parable, says Zossima, lies in the fact that it is a mystery, "that the passing earthly show and the eternal verity are brought together." This, of course, is diametrically opposed to what Ivan believes. He refuses to accept any idea that cannot be comprehended by earthly logic. But for Zossima, the greatness of God lies in the fact that man cannot comprehend God's ways and that some things of earth must remain a mystery. Only with such a mystery does man realize the full extent of God's glory. If man could comprehend all, then God would lose his sense of majesty. And, again in contrast to Ivan (who loves humanity but cannot accept the idea of suffering that God imposes upon man), Zossima says "one who does not believe in God will not believe in God's people. He who believes in God's people will see His Holiness too, even though he had not believed in it till then." The elder insists on practicing active love for mankind; only through love will one come to believe in God. For the present, Ivan would disagree. He spends his time intellectualizing over abstruse problems; he has no time left for active love.

With the appearance of the mysterious stranger, Zossima is put to his first test. It would have been easy to tell the stranger that he has suffered enough and that there is no need for him to ruin his life and his family's life by making an open confession. But Zossima is quietly persuasive in his efforts to get the stranger to recognize his errors. There is no attempt at coercion, but simply a quiet plea for him to perform that which his conscience tells him must be done.

As Zossima confides his wisdom to Alyosha, the reader should be aware that the elder's views are essentially those by which Dostoevsky himself tried to live, or at least, wished to live by. Particularly, Dostoevsky was interested in these concepts:

1. *The Russian monk and his possible significance.* — Zossima believes that the salvation of Russia would come from two sources — the Russian monks and from a vast, idealized section of the Russian population that he referred to as the Russian people, or the Russian folk. The monks, however, were even more important than the folk if the regeneration of Russia was to be accomplished. From the monks would come the energy and ideas of purity and love. The monk, Zossima believes, practices obedience, fasting, and prayer, believing that these three

disciplines will accomplish for him the only true freedom: sacred freedom. Such freedom is forever denied the man who exists in contemporary society, the slave to mechanical and material frivolities; he will never attain the freedom needed for a pure understanding of life's meaning. He is too involved with life to be able to contemplate life. Only the monk, a man who has "freed himself from the tyranny of material things and habits" can conceive great ideas and serve them. In essence, this is the elder's answer to the question posed by the Grand Inquisitor and Ivan. Only in freedom can man conceive of ideas great enough to make life worth preserving.

And after the monk gives birth to example and philosophy, the renascence begins and, within the Russian folk, a new Russia is nourished. The folk, of course, can never hope to completely emulate the life of the monk but, because of their living close to the soil and to basic matters of life, they can most easily assimilate the wisdom of the Russian monk. Of course Zossima realizes that the average peasant sins occasionally, but he also believes that the peasant realizes that he is wrong in his sinning. This realization will be his salvation, for man must first recognize righteousness as the supreme virtue; this the folk do. One must not despair of the peasant, Zossima counsels, for even in his sinfulness and in his ignorant ways, "salvation will come from the people, from their faith and their meekness," an idea very often advocated by Dostoevsky. He uses, for example, Sonia in *Crime and Punishment* as such a type, the so-called passive redemptive character, and suggests that through the passive acceptance of faith and by extreme meekness, salvation will be achieved. The folk are Zossima's hope, for they believe basically as does the monk. The elder says that "an unbelieving reformer will never do anything in Russia. Even if he is sincere in heart and a genius, the people will meet the atheist and overcome him." But if one considers the widespread atheism that followed the Communist revolution in Russia, Dostoevsky perhaps never wrote anything that proved to be so absolutely incorrect as this prophecy of Father Zossima.

2. *Of masters and servants, and of whether it is possible for them to be brothers in spirit.* — Zossima advocates an absolute equality for all men. True dignity does not come from the possession of great material wealth. Dignity, the elder says, is derived only from an inner sense of personal worth; it is able to respect another person without envying that person. When man attains such dignity he creates a unity, a brotherhood in which a master may associate with a servant without losing either self-respect or dignity. This is Zossima's utopia, founded upon "the grand unity of man," preserved by men who long with all their heart to be the servant of all.

3. *Of prayer, of love and of contact with other worlds.* — Zossima admonished his adherents to pray for others, even those who have sinned. God, he says, will look favorably upon any sinner who stands before Him, proving that someone is offering up a prayer for that sinner. And again the elder re-emphasizes to those assembled his strong belief in the power of positive love. "Love a man even in his sin, for that is the semblance of Divine Love and is the highest love on earth. Love all God's creation, the whole and every grain of sand in it. Love every leaf, every ray of God's light. Love the animals, love the plants, love everything. If you love everything, you will perceive the divine mystery in things." By loving, man gains new respect for everything in God's world. Thus "we must love not occasionally, for a moment, but for ever."

One of Zossima's principal ideas that particularly touches Alyosha is the elder's view of man's responsibility for another's sins. Zossima maintains that everyone must make himself "responsible for all men's sins... for as soon as you sincerely make yourself responsible for everything and for all men, you will see at once that it is really so and that you are to blame for every one and for all things." If one carries this idea to its logical conclusion, then, we see that Alyosha must eventually take partial responsibility for the murder of his father. This he indeed does, finally realizing that man must become an active participant rather than a passive observer of life.

Concerning man's limitation of understanding all that is holy, Zossima says that man is given a mystic sense of his loving bond with the other world. Like Ivan, the elder admits that man cannot understand the mysterious ways of God, but, for Zossima, the very existence of something so mysteriously unexplainable is proof that man owes love and allegiance to a higher power. Zossima takes Ivan's premises, therefore, for his proof of God's existence. "On the final judgment," says the elder, "man will not be asked to account for things which he cannot comprehend, but only for those things he understands."

4. *Can a man judge his fellow creatures?* — Zossima believes that no one can judge a criminal. First, one must recognize that no man is only a criminal and perhaps more than all other men, the seemingly innocent, and not the allegedly guilty, is most to blame for whatever crime has been committed. Alyosha uses such a theory when he refuses to judge Dmitri; furthermore, during his brother's trial, he forgives him. From a realistic point of view, Zossima's views on the criminal are too ideal. Zossima would allow a criminal to go free and hope that he would come to condemn his acts. Such idealism is touchingly naive.

And with the same sort of idealism, Zossima advocates kissing the earth, "love it with an unceasing, consuming love." Love of the mother earth, one might note, is central to many of Dostoevsky's novels. In *Crime and Punishment*, the murderer Raskolnikov is told to go and bow down to the earth which he has defiled because of his crime. And, in the poem from Schiller that Dmitri often recites, there is a hymn of praise for the earthly existence. In total loving then—loving even the earth—Zossima says that man can realize an ecstasy which is a "gift of God," not given to many but certainly to the elect. The ideal of a spiritual elite is foreign to Ivan's thinking, but Zossima believes in such a minority and stresses that they should be proud of being elect; their examples will lead others to God's light.

5. *Of hell and hell fire, a mystic reflection.*—Zossima's views on this subject do not conform with the orthodox views of the church and later Ferapont will allude to this fact when he drives the devils from Zossima's cell. Zossima absolutely does not believe in a material hell fire, one that burns and punishes. To him, hell is spiritual agony, growing out of the inner conscience of the damned. If there were material punishment, he says, it would alleviate the spiritual punishment because of its intense physical pain. The greater punishment, the spiritual punishment, is the sinner's recognition that he is forever separated from God. Zossima strays even further from the teachings of the church by his prayers for the condemned. He prays for them because "love can never be an offense to Christ."

PART THREE

BOOK VII

Summary

As soon as Father Zossima's body is prepared for burial, it is placed in a large room and, news traveling fast, the room is quickly filled. As soon as they hear of the elder's death, large numbers of people gather, expecting a miracle. There is no miracle, however, only this: Zossima's corpse begins to putrify almost immediately and the odor of decay is soon sickening to all of the mourners. All present become nauseated and begin to grow fearful because they believe that the decay of a body is related to its spiritual character. It seems an evil omen that Zossima's corpse would rot so soon after death, for the elder was popularly believed to be on the verge of sainthood.

Discontented monks and enemies of Father Zossima are not long
to act. Quickly they announce that the decaying body is proof that the
elder was no saint; at last the doctrine he preached is proved to be incorrect. The townspeople are confused. Tradition and superstition are
embedded in their nerves. They have expected something awesome but
certainly not a portent that points to Zossima's being a possible disciple
of Satan. Not even Alyosha escapes the fear that grips the community.
He cannot understand why God has allowed such disgrace to accompany
the elder's death.

Father Ferapont, the fanatical ascetic, rushes to Zossima's cell and
begins to exorcise devils out of all the corners, and elsewhere there
is also madness—the entire monastery is torn by confused loyalities
and uncertainties. Finally, the extreme Ferapont is ordered to leave.
But shortly thereafter there is another departure from the monastery.
Alyosha leaves also; he wishes to find solitude to grieve and ponder.

Alone, he again questions the justice of all that has happened. Instead of receiving the glory that Alyosha believed was Zossima's due,
his mentor is now "degraded and dishonored." Alyosha cannot doubt
God, but he must question why He has allowed such a dreadful thing
to occur.

Alyosha is interrupted in his thoughts as the seminarian, Rakitin,
who earlier mocked Alyosha, ridicules his grief and makes contemptu-
ous remarks about Zossima's decaying body. He tempts Alyosha with
sausage and vodka, both of which are denied a monk during Lent, and
Alyosha suddenly accepts both. Rakitin then goes a step further and
suggests that they visit Grushenka and again Alyosha agrees.

Grushenka is astonished at her visitors but regains her composure
and explains that she is waiting for an important message to arrive.
They are curious about the message and she tells them that it comes
from an army officer whom she loved five years ago and who deserted
her. Now he has returned to the province and is sending for her.

Grushenka notices Alyosha's dejection and tries to cheer him by
sitting on his knee and teasing him, but when she learns that Father
Zossima has died only a few hours earlier, she too becomes remorseful.
She upbraids herself and denounces her life as that of a wicked sinner.
Alyosha stops her, speaking with great kindness and understanding, and
the two suddenly exchange glimpses into each other's souls. Love and
trust are given, one to the other, and Grushenka unabashedly speaks to

Alyosha of her problems; she no longer feels ashamed of her life. As for Alyosha, Grushenka's genuine expressions of sympathy lift him out of the deep depression he has felt since Zossima's death. Rakitin cannot understand this sudden compassion between them and is spiteful and vindictive, especially after Grushenka confesses that she had paid Rakitin to bring Alyosha to her. The message arrives from Grushenka's lover and she excuses herself and leaves, asking Alyosha to tell Dmitri that she did love him—once, for an hour.

Very late Alyosha returns to the monastery and goes to Zossima's cell. He kneels and prays, still troubled by many things, then hears Father Paissy reading the account of the wedding at Cana in the Gospel of St. John and, because he is exhausted and because of the sweet lull of the Father's voice, Alyosha dozes. He dreams that he is at the marriage in Cana, along with Christ and the other guests. Zossima appears and calls to Alyosha; he tells him to come forth and join the crowd, reminding him that man should be joyful. Even today, he says, Alyosha has helped Grushenka find her path toward salvation.

Alyosha wakes and his eyes are filled with tears of joy. He goes outside and flings himself on the earth, kissing and embracing it. His heart is filled with ecstasy over his new knowledge and his new understanding of the joy of life.

Commentary

Dostoevsky has been preparing the reader throughout the novel for this single crisis in Alyosha's life. There have been many hints that a miracle is expected to accompany Zossima's death, but one of the central points of Ivan's Grand Inquisitor tale is that man must believe freely in the teachings of a person without the benefit of either divine manifestations or miracles. A person's beliefs, furthermore, can be greatly strengthened by emerging triumphantly from a period of great doubt. And, in this chapter, Dostoevsky presents Alyosha's tests—corollaries of Christ's tests in the wilderness. If Alyosha emerges successfully, he will then be qualified to move within society and to influence it.

Alyosha, of course, does not need miracles for himself. But he recognizes the need of others for them and with no miracle and because the body is decaying, he knows that spiteful rumors will rise around Zossima's memory. He cannot endure the holiest of holy men exposed to jeering and mockery. Such indignity and humiliation of premature decay are unnecessary.

Alyosha's questionings align him closely with his brother Ivan. Ivan also asked about God's justice and, like his brother, Alyosha does not question God; he is concerned only about His justice. When the seminarian appears, Alyosha even echos Ivan's arguments by saying, "I am not rebelling against my God; I simply don't accept His world." But Karamazovs are concerned with justice, not God Himself.

Alyosha, of course, realizes that Christ went through such jeering and mockery. But, for a moment, he gives way to temptation and, in this way, he becomes human and not semi-divine; he becomes believably mortal. He can later be more deeply admired for his courage in resisting temptation. Alyosha questions and by his questions one realizes the value of doubting. A serene acceptance of all — with no questioning — is neither courageous nor admirable; it is merely shallow, immature. Alyosha, when he defies his vows and accepts the sausage and vodka and goes to see Grushenka, has a temporary spiritual revolt, but emerges a much stronger adherent of faith.

In terms of a larger perspective within the total action of the novel, one should remember that Ivan leaves town on the day that Zossima dies. Ivan catches the train about the same time that Alyosha arrives at Grushenka's. Also, it is later this evening that Fyodor's murder takes place and it is also later this evening that Alyosha rediscovers his faith and rededicates himself to the principles advocated by Father Zossima.

Ironically, Alyosha's transformation initially results from his encounter with Grushenka. He goes there in defiance of his monastic orders and Grushenka, for her part, hopes to seduce Alyosha's innocence; his purity is threatening. But when they meet, Alyosha sees in Grushenka a woman he cannot condemn; he sees "a loving heart" that can compassionately respond to the suffering Alyosha is undergoing. In his confession to her, he admits that he came hoping only to find an evil woman. Such honesty is infectious and transforming. Grushenka says, "He is the first, the only one who has pitied me...I've been waiting all my life for some one like you. I knew that some one like you would come and forgive me." And, unlikely as it seems, perhaps in a way like the miracle that all expected, carnality and purity create new love and compassion. The explanation, however, is far from being that of a miracle. Alyosha has only followed Zossima's teachings. He has loved Grushenka; he has not damned her and he, and she, suddenly rediscover themselves.

At the end of this scene, Rakitin, who could not understand the attraction between Alyosha and Grushenka, feels that Alyosha dislikes him for taking twenty-five rubles from Grushenka. But the point is this: Alyosha does not judge him; Rakitin leaves because he judges himself and finds himself guilty.

When Alyosha returns to the monastery, he feels such mixed emotions that there is a "sweetness in his heart." By this single experience with Grushenka, he has found the value of much that Zossima has preached. He has seen how responding to even such a person as Grushenka has changed his entire view of life. Suddenly, he feels himself at peace with the entire world.

Alyosha listens to the monk read of the marriage in Cana and realizes that Christ came to give people pleasure in this world; he came to preach a message of joy and love. This is exactly what Father Zossima advocated. In his dream, he sees his beloved elder in the presence of Christ and knows that the message they both preached is far more important than any "miracle." With love, he embraces the earth and is quietly filled with new understanding of all Zossima has said. He leaves the monastery with new conviction. He is ready at last to take his place in the world as Zossima has said that he must.

BOOK VIII

Summary

Dmitri feels that there is still a possibility that Grushenka may accept him as her husband, but his problem is that if she does accept him, he cannot rightfully carry her away until he repays the money he owes Katerina Ivanovna. In a desperate effort to find a solution, then, he contrives a fantastic scheme. He goes to old Samsonov — Grushenka's previous protector — and offers him the rights to some property that he believes the law courts might take away from Fyodor and give to him if the old merchant will immediately give him 3,000 rubles. The merchant, of course, refuses and plays a trick on Dmitri: he sends him off to the country to see a merchant named Lyagavy, who is bargaining with Fyodor for this very property.

Dmitri pawns his watch, hires transportation to the neighboring town, and finds the merchant. Unfortunately, the man is thoroughly drunk. Dmitri tries to sober him up, but is unable to, so waits until the next day. The merchant remains in a stupor, so Dmitri returns to town, hoping to borrow money from Madame Hohlakov. Madame Hohlakov, however, tries to convince him that he should go off to the gold mines if he wants money; she absolutely refuses to lend him anything.

Dmitri next goes to claim Grushenka, but finds that she is not at home. The servant is no help; she pretends that she does not know where Grushenka has gone. Dmitri is outraged. He picks up a brass pestle and dashes to his father's house. Then he sneaks into the garden and peers through a lighted window. He is sure that Grushenka has finally come to the old man. He is disappointed, however; he sees only his father pacing the floor. But to make certain that Grushenka is not there, Dmitri taps the secret signal. The old man opens the window and Dmitri is greatly relieved. Grushenka is not with his father!

Meanwhile, Grigory, the old servant, awakens and goes into the garden for a breath of air. He sees Dmitri leaving the garden and tries to stop him, but Dmitri, confused and distraught, fights off his attacker and finally strikes him on the head with the pestle. The servant crumples to the ground and Dmitri stops a moment to see if the man is dead. He tries to stop the puddle of blood; then, in panic he tosses the pestle away and flees.

He returns to Grushenka's house and forces the servants to reveal where Grushenka has gone. The answer is agonizing: she has gone to rejoin her first lover. Dmitri knows now that he can no longer claim the girl. He must step aside and leave her to her happiness. But he passionately wants one last look at Grushenka. After that, he will kill himself; his future holds nothing without Grushenka. He goes to retrieve pistols from Perhotin, a minor official who lent Dmitri money and kept the pistols as security. Perhotin is amazed to see Dmitri, who is now carrying a large bundle of money and blotched with blood. He goes to a nearby store with young Karamazov and remains while Dmitri buys three hundred rubles worth of food and wine and makes arrangements to go where Grushenka is rumored to be staying. After Perhotin watches Dmitri leave, he decides to do some detective work.

Dmitri is in luck: Grushenka is indeed staying where he was directed. He rushes to her rooms and greatly shocks Grushenka but she recovers and welcomes him. Until now the celebration has been very gloomy and restrained. Dmitri's wine helps liven the spirits and soon Grushenka and her officer friend and Dmitri are all playing cards together. All does not go well, however. The Polish officer begins to cheat and tosses out disgusting, cynical remarks. Grushenka recoils. She realizes that she can never love such a man. Dmitri senses Grushenka's pain and when the officer finally turns his insults on her, Dmitri forces him into another room and locks him inside. Then a real celebration ensues and Grushenka knows that she can love only Dmitri.

Dmitri is not quite so lucky. He is troubled because he has struck Grigory, perhaps killed him; he also owes money to Katerina Ivanovna. He talks with Grushenka of their future together but they are interrupted. A group of officers arrive, charge Dmitri with the murder of his father, and place him under arrest.

Commentary

Until now, the novel has moved with a sure, slow deliberateness as Dostoevsky depicted the intellectual conflicts in Ivan, the philosophy of Zossima, and the mystic affirmation of life by Alyosha. Now, however, this section, devoted to Dmitri, rushes along with breath-taking speed as it records Dmitri's frantic efforts to save both his life and his love.

Dostoevsky is a master at depicting the torment of despondency within a character who has no money and desperately needs it in order to salvage some remnant of his honor. Dmitri has spent most of the money that Katerina Ivanovna has lent him and, although we know that he has the rest concealed on him, he still feels that he cannot elope with Grushenka until the entire sum is repaid. He must secure the money so that he can begin a new life with Grushenka and still retain his integrity. If he were to use Katerina's money to elope with Grushenka, he feels that this would be his absolute lowest, most degrading act. And, looking forward, when he decides to step aside and allow Grushenka to return to her first love, one should realize that by this time, he has decided to end his life. This resolution should be kept in mind when Dmitri shows few qualms about usurping the money; it is not that he considers it any less dishonorable but, because he intends to take his life, he will not have to face the dishonor.

Dostoevsky does not present an entirely admirable character in Dmitri. He continually lets the reader know that Dmitri's financial predicament is due to his irresponsibility with money. Consequently, his frantic search for someone who will lend him money and his absurd proposals reveal his lack of acumen. He is also unable to realize that the old merchant, Samsonov, is making fun of him and sending him on a wild goose chase. It takes two days for Dmitri to come to his senses, but even then he still tries to convince Madame Hohlakov that she should lend him money. Were he more rational he would know that the lady thoroughly detests him. These scenes of begging, then, show to what degree of desperation Dmitri will go in his need for money. This alone casts suspicion upon him concerning his father's murder.

Remember, too, that Dostoevsky arranges his plot in such a way that it is natural and logical for the reader to assume on first reading that Dmitri is the murderer. Every detail in this chapter attests to the incriminating evidence that will be accumulated against Dmitri. Furthermore, even Dmitri's thoughts cast suspicion upon him. As he goes to see Madame Hohlakov, for example, he thinks "...his last hope...if this broke down, nothing else was left him in the world but to rob and murder some one for the three thousand." Such evidence, coupled with his distraught emotions, allows the reader to assume that Dmitri is indeed guilty of his father's murder.

Ironically, one small lie contributes most of all to Dmitri's arrest. Fenya, Grushenka's servant, lies to him; she says she does not know of Grushenka's whereabouts, thereby forcing Dmitri to go to his father's to search for her. Had the servant told the truth, then Dmitri would not have been present at the scene of the murder; nor would he have been covered with Grigory's blood.

Dmitri's resolve to commit suicide is quite believable. On the road to Mokroe to meet Grushenka, he fully intends to see her, then kill himself. Indeed, the mere fact that he is now spending the rest of Katerina Ivanovna's money and the fact that he has left old Grigory to face possible death from his wounds all suggest that Dmitri has no longer any concern about the future. During the ride, he knows that he cannot stand in Grushenka's way but he wants to see her once more. He is in agony; he even asks the peasant driver, as one might ask a priest, to forgive him all the sins of his life. Incidentally, with this last act, he echoes one of Zossima's ideas concerning the repudiation of master-servant distinction and the responsibility of all men for one another.

Dmitri fully intends to kill himself and his prayer, most of all, reveals the anguish in his soul. "Lord," he pleads, "receive me with all my lawlessness and do not condemn me. Let me pass Thy judgment – do not condemn me for I have condemned myself...for I love Thee, O Lord. I am a wretch, but I love Thee. If Thou sendest me to hell, I shall love Thee there and from there I shall cry out that I love Thee for ever and ever." In this prayer is Dmitri's most redeeming value; it holds the key to Dmitri's character—that which Zossima recognized. Dmitri is one of the "folk" of whom the elder spoke. He is one of those who may sin, but who still love God. That love, said Zossima, leads to salvation; such deep love the elder recognized early in his relationship with Dmitri. Henceforth young Karamazov calls upon this love and its strength as he begins the slow journey toward regeneration and redemption.

BOOK IX

Summary

Perhotin's curiosity is overwhelming. He cannot but be suspicious of Dmitri, so decides to investigate the truth of Dmitri's explanations. He goes to Grushenka's maid and learns about the brass pestle, then goes to Madame Hohlakov's to confirm Dmitri's story about the money. Madame Hohlakov is annoyed at being awakened so late at night, but on hearing the reason, she excitedly declares that she has never given anything to Dmitri.

Perhotin has no choice; it is his duty to report all that has happened to the police. But when he arrives, he finds that others also have news to report to the police. Marfa has sent word to them that Fyodor has been murdered.

An investigation follows and it is decided that Dmitri Karamazov must be immediately apprehended. Dmitri is arrested and pleads that he is innocent of the crime but no one, of course, believes him—not even Grushenka, who bursts into the room crying that she drove him to commit murder but that she will love him forever. On cross-examination, Dmitri confesses that he is guilty of hating his father but he maintains that in spite of this, he did not murder the old man. His guilt, however, now seems more definite to the authorities. Eventually more admissions are made by Dmitri and he confesses that he did know of the 3,000 rubles that his father had. And he admits that he was indeed in desperate need of that exact sum to repay his debt to Katerina Ivanovna. He does not try to conceal facts that seem to implicate him in the murder, and the knot tightens. Questioned more carefully about his activities on the night of the murder, Dmitri accounts for all his moves, including the visit to his father's house. He even admits taking the pestle with him but cannot give an explanation as to why he did. He is completely honest—on all but one matter: the origin of the large sum of money he had when arrested.

Dmitri is ordered to undress and submit to a thorough search. The officers go through his clothes, searching for more money, and find additional blood stains; they decide to retain his clothing as evidence. Dmitri is then forced to realize the seriousness of his situation and tells where the money came from. He explains about the orgy with Grushenka and reveals that he actually spent only half of the 3,000 rubles Katerina gave him; the other half he has saved. But, having decided to commit suicide, he saw no value in the money any longer and decided to use it for one last fling.

Other witnesses are called in and all agree that Dmitri has stated several times that he spent 3,000 rubles on the orgy and needed 3,000 to replace the sum.

When Grushenka is brought in for her testimony, Dmitri swears to her that he is not the murderer. She, in turn, tries to convince the officials that he is telling the truth, but she is sure that they do not believe her.

The officials complete their examination of witnesses, then inform Dmitri that they have arrived at a decision: he must be retained in prison. He is allowed to say goodby to Grushenka, however. Deeply apologetic for the trouble he has caused her, Dmitri asks her forgiveness and Grushenka answers by promising to remain by him forever.

Commentary

In this book all of Dmitri's past lies and braggadaccios coalesce and smother his pleas of innocence. Logically, one could say that Dmitri had the motive for the murder and was, as confessed, even at the scene of the crime. The conclusion seems obvious. Dostoevsky has carefully arranged the details and the circumstances in such a manner that the case against Dmitri is wholly convincing; the man is guilty. But there is another dimension to the investigation. As the officers review Dmitri's life, Dmitri also reviews his life and begins to realize the nature of his past and its meaning. It is this realization that greatly aids his reformation. Only in the light of such dire circumstances is it possible for someone like Dmitri to evaluate all his acts and take full responsibility for them.

Grushenka has never spoken with Father Zossima, but the wisdom of the elder is a part of her newly discovered self. She tries, for example, to take the blame — to take Dmitri's sins upon herself — by crying out that she is responsible for the crime. She played with the passions of an old man and his son and, as a result, murder was committed. Later, when Dmitri swears to her that he is innocent, she is convinced of the truth of what he has said. She needs no other proof; this alone illustrates the extent of her love for Dmitri. This is the deeply transforming love that Zossima taught.

At first, Dmitri thinks it only a matter of time before he will be able to convince the officials of his innocence, but as the questions and the evidence begin to mount and tighten around him, he begins to see the seriousness of his position. It is then that he undergoes a change. He realizes the need for a transformation. He confesses almost every detail of his life and is bitterly ashamed. And because the officials are writing down the sorry details of his past, he is even more deeply ashamed.

He is quick to see that he is not guilty of the murder but that he is indeed guilty. So often he boasted of killing his father and so often he wished for his father's death; now all that is on trial and he stands, literally, naked before the probing magistrates. The shame of his entire life is revealed in all its disgusting corruptness.

In many of his novels, Dostoevsky is concerned with the actions of police—how officials conduct investigations. Dostoevsky especially details what questions are asked. And throughout the interrogation of Dmitri Karamazov, Dostoevsky does not distort the processes of justice. The officials are depicted as honest and penetrating men, finally arriving at a reasonable conclusion. Dmitri is not tried by brutally caricatured sadists. The logic of the evidence exists.

There is a bit of irony in Dmitri's consideration of Smerdyakov. He is positive that the murder could not have been committed by the cook. He is, according to Dmitri, "a man of the most abject character and a coward."

Perhaps Dmitri's most redeeming act is this: he judges himself and finally welcomes the suffering to be imposed upon him. He assumes his share of the guilt for the murder of his father and he assumes the responsibility for all the deeds of his past. Exclaiming to the officials, he says, "I tell you again, with a bleeding heart, I have learnt a great deal this night. I have learnt that it's not only impossible to live a scoundrel, but impossible to die a scoundrel."

Dmitri's dream is further proof of his redemption. When he dreams that he is crossing the steppes on a cold winter day, passing through a burned village, a gaunt peasant woman holds a crying baby in her arms and Dmitri's heart overflows with anguish and sympathy for such poor people. He is overcome with compassion and love for these and for all humanity. Thus when he wakes he is ready to accept his suffering and exclaims, "By suffering I shall be purified." He is ready to undergo a period of trial and emerge a new and responsible character.

PART FOUR

BOOK X

Summary

Kolya Krassotkin, a widow's only child, is a mature and independent thirteen-year-old with a reputation for being exceptionally daring and imprudent. He is also the boy whom earlier Ilusha stabbed with a penknife; but, good-naturedly, Kolya has never held a grudge. At present he has been training a dog, Perezvon, to do complicated tricks.

On the day before Dmitri's trial, young Kolya is staying with two children of his mother's tenant. He feels uneasy because he has an urgent errand to attend to and leaves as soon as the servant returns. His errand turns out to be a visit to Ilusha. Kolya knows that Alyosha has arranged for other boys to visit the dying Ilusha every day, but until today Kolya has never visited the boy.

He arrives at Ilusha's with a friend, Smurov, and asks him to call Alyosha outside; he has a great curiosity to meet Alyosha. The two meet and immediately become good friends, especially because Alyosha treats Kolya as an equal. Kolya explains to his new friend about Ilusha's background and tells him that once they were fast friends, but when Kolya heard that Ilusha fed a dog a piece of bread with a pin in it, he tried to punish the boy. The punishment backfired, however, and Kolya was stabbed with the penknife. Since this happened, however, Ilusha has come to feel very bad about the dog, Zhutchka.

Alyosha takes Kolya inside and Ilusha is overjoyed to see his old friend again. Kolya, however, begins to tease Ilusha about the dog; then, before anyone can stop him, he calls in the dog he has been training. It turns out to be Zhutchka. Everyone is delighted and the dying Ilusha sheds tears of happiness. Kolya explains that, until now, he has stayed away so that he could train the dog for Ilusha.

A doctor from Moscow, whom Katerina has sent for, arrives to examine Ilusha and the visitors reluctantly leave the room. As they wait outside, Kolya explains his views of life to Alyosha and Alyosha listens carefully, understanding the boy's real motives. He wants to impress Alyosha with his hodgepodge of other people's philosophies. Alyosha is sympathetic to him, though, and especially drawn to the young boy when he confesses his weaknesses.

As the doctor leaves, it is quite apparent that Ilusha has not long to live. Even Ilusha is aware that he is dying. He tries to comfort his father, and Kolya is deeply affected by this scene between father and son. He promises Alyosha that he will now come often to visit the dying boy.

Commentary

Some critics have complained that in a novel of such extreme complexity and length, Book X does not contribute to the novel's unity. The section has often been said to be superfluous and a flaw in construction. A reader, they say, is anxiously concerned about Dmitri at this point, not about Ilusha. But, because of the heavy chapters of violence and passion and murder, this section can be explained in terms of Dostoevsky's inserting a healthy bit of youthful fresh air. The reader is relieved from the strain of contemplating Dmitri's fate.

This relief, however, does not explain all the charges leveled against this section of the novel. It does not, for example, explain an obvious change in tone. Here, Dostoevsky inserts the most overt sentimentality in the entire novel. He seems to play with the reader's emotions and much of the pathetic background material of young Kolya's life is not central to the novel except in the very large perspective of establishing him as the person whom Alyosha will train and who will become one of Russia's future citizens, entrusted with the ideas of Father Zossima.

Perhaps, however, the real purpose of the section is this: Dostoevsky is showing Alyosha as he moves among Russian youth, quietly influencing their lives as a living example of Father Zossima's philosophy. The hope of Russia lies in the young and in the common people and Alyosha teaches Kolya much in this section. He meets him as an equal and offers him understanding and trust; he teaches Kolya that one cannot judge Ilusha's father, saying that there are people of rare character who have been crushed by life. The buffoonery of Ilusha's father, he says, is only the man's way of being ironic toward those who have humiliated and intimidated him for years.

Alyosha also instructs Kolya in what a man can learn from another. And because Alyosha accepts all as equals, even Kolya, he kindles a responsive chord of love. By his quiet examples, Alyosha corrects immature views without arousing animosity. He is, for example, careful not to denounce Kolya's potpourri of philosophy; instead, he simply explains that although he disagrees, he does not have contempt for Kolya's ideas. By the latter's response, it is obvious that he will become one of the strongest disciples of Alyosha.

BOOK XI

Summary

During the two months since Dmitri was arrested, Grushenka has been ill and now, as she begins to recover physically, there are also signs of a major spiritual recovery, of a complete "spiritual transformation in her." Also, there is another change: she and Alyosha have become fast friends, and she confides to him that she and Dmitri have quarreled again. In addition, she fears that Dmitri is once again falling in love with Katerina Ivanova. What most concerns her, however, is that Dmitri and Ivan are concealing a secret from her. She pleads with Alyosha to discover what the secret is. Again, Alyosha promises to help a human being in trouble.

On his way to question Dmitri, Alyosha stops and visits Lise, whom he finds feverish and excited. She tells him that she longs to be punished and castigated by God, and says that she regularly prays to suffer torture, for she can no longer respect anything nor anyone. She continuously feels possessed with a terrible urge to destroy. The young girl becomes hysterical as she confesses her secret thoughts, then suddenly sends Alyosha away. And, after he leaves, she does a curious thing: she intentionally slams the door on her fingers and calls herself a wretch.

When Alyosha arrives at the prison where Dmitri is being held, he notices that Rakitin, a seminarian acquaintance, is leaving. He asks Dmitri about Rakitin's visit and is told that the seminarian hopes to write an article proving that Dmitri is the victim of an unhappy environment and that he could not help killing his father. Dmitri then explains to the puzzled Alyosha that he does not take Rakitin seriously, that he tolerates him only because he is amused by his "advanced ideas." More seriously, Dmitri confesses that he now understands his responsibility for his past life and sins and that he is ready to suffer and do penance for his sins. He is sure that there can still be a full and rewarding life for him. Only one thing troubles him, however — Grushenka. He is afraid that the authorities will not let her accompany him to Siberia and he fears that without Grushenka he will be unable to face his years of punishment and thus will never be redeemed.

Dmitri also tells Alyosha that Ivan has come to the prison and has given him a plan for escape. Of course, Dmitri says, Ivan believes him guilty of murder. He then turns to Alyosha and asks his brother's opinion. Never before has he had the courage to speak so candidly with Alyosha and when he hears the young many say, "I've never for one instant believed that you were the murderer," Dmitri is greatly relieved. He feels the power of a new life rising in him.

Alyosha leaves Dmitri and goes to Katerina shortly thereafter. He finds Ivan just leaving but his brother remains long enough to hear what Alyosha says concerning Dmitri. When Ivan leaves, Katerina becomes highly emotional and insists that Alyosha follow him; she is convinced that Ivan is going mad.

Alyosha rushes to rejoin Ivan and learns yet another piece of news. Ivan says that Katerina has a "document in her hands...that proves conclusively" that Dmitri did indeed murder their father. Alyosha denies that such a document could exist and Ivan then asks who the murderer is. Alyosha tells him, "it wasn't you who killed Father," explaining that he is aware that Ivan has been accusing himself, but that God has sent Alyosha to Ivan to reassure him. Ivan is sickened by Alyosha's religious mysticism and leaves him abruptly.

Ivan's nausea, however, is not due wholly to his brother's mysticism; the sickness begins earlier, almost simultaneously with his first visit to Smerdyakov. The servant is recovering in the hospital and maintains that his epileptic seizure on the night of the murder was real. He says further that he understood that Ivan went to Moscow because he suspected a murder was about to be committed and wanted to be far from the scene of the crime. Ivan answers that he will not reveal to the authorities that Smerdyakov is able to sham an epileptic seizure and Smerdyakov counters by promising to say nothing of a certain conversation, their last before the murder.

During Ivan's second visit with Smerdyakov, he demands to know what Smerdyakov meant by his strange statement about their last conversation prior to the murder. Smerdyakov explains that Ivan so desired his father's death, in order to come into a large portion of the inheritance, that he planned to leave and thereby silently assented to Fyodor's murder.

Ivan leaves, bewildered, half realizing that he must share the guilt if Smerdyakov murdered Fyodor. He goes to see Katerina and explains his complicity and his guilt and Katerina is able to temporarily alleviate some of his anxiety. She shows him a letter that Dmitri wrote to her saying that, if necessary, he would kill Fyodor in order to repay the money he stole from her. This letter puts Ivan's mind at ease; Dmitri, not Smerdyakov, is surely the villain.

Ivan does not see Smerdyakov again until the night before the trial but by this time the Karamazov servant is tired of all pretense. He openly admits that it was he who killed Fyodor. He stoutly maintains, though, that he did not act alone; he acted only as an instrument of Ivan, saying, "It was following your words I did it." He then explains in great detail how he accomplished the murder, continuously referring to the dual responsibility for the murder. Smerdyakov furthermore recalls all the philosophical discussions the two men have had and accuses Ivan of having given him the moral justification that made it possible. All this Ivan did, he says, besides leaving town and permitting the act.

Stunned, Ivan returns to his lodgings; he plans to reveal at the trial next day all that Smerdyakov has told him, but in his room he finds a devil. The apparition is dressed like a rather shoddy middle-aged gentleman and is full of cynical criticism. He forces Ivan to face the most terrifying aspects of his inner secrets, taunting him with his private fears and weaknesses until finally Ivan goes mad with rage and hurls a cup at the intruder. At that moment he hears Alyosha knocking at the window. His brother brings the news that Smerdyakov has just hanged himself. Ivan is so upset by his "devil" that when he tries to tell Alyosha about the experience, he cannot. Alyosha discovers to his horror that Ivan is suffering a nervous breakdown. He stays the night to nurse his brother.

Commentary

This book is concerned primarily with depicting Ivan's guilt and with detailing his duplicity in the murder of his father. Particularly, Dostoevsky emphasizes the three interviews with Smerdyakov (solving for the reader, on the plot level, the mystery of Fyodor's killer) and

Ivan's conversation with his imaginary devil. Dostoevsky manipulates the attention of the reader away from the plot question of legal guilt and confronts him with the intricacies of Ivan's dilemma about metaphysical guilt.

Also, in Book XI, Dostoevsky provides necessary background concerning what has happened during the two months that Dmitri has been in jail and it is most important to the author's total view that one know that Grushenka has lain ill following the arrest of Dmitri. One of Dostoevsky's prime concepts, prominent in all his novels, is that crime (or involvement with crime) is often accompanied by illness. And, besides Grushenka's falling ill after she realizes her role in the Karamazov crime, Ivan also falls desperately ill upon his realization of his involvement in the murder. Thus, besides coupling crime and illness, Dostoevsky is structuring a much more important tenet. Because Grushenka is ill and suffers, she becomes regenerated. Knowledge through suffering is one of the novel's prime equations. And to underscore his presentation, Dostoevsky, as a contrast to the sensitive Grushenka, records the mincings of the whimsical and impish Lise. This young lady maintains that she needs to suffer in order to learn and that she likes to make other people suffer, but she is both shallow and superficial. Suffering, for example, is defined by her as punishing children by eating pineapple compote before them. She punishes herself by slamming the door on her finger!

This destructive girl turns Dostoevsky's theories inside out and delights in reviling everyone and everything. Her perversity functions as a vivid contrast to the more healthy and sound soul of Grushenka.

In Chapter 4, the continued regeneration of Dmitri is recorded. Currently, he ponders Ivan's offer of escape and the finances necessary to accomplish it. Earlier he might have impulsively fled; now, however, he has developed into a type of Zossima-man. He feels that he is "responsible for all." "I go for all," he says, "because one must go for all. I didn't kill Father, but I've got to go. I accept it." Furthermore, he now believes that life is full of enjoyment even if one must live imprisoned. His dilemma therefore is this: he wants to accept his suffering and he looks forward to salvation through suffering but he knows that he cannot withstand suffering unless Grushenka is beside him, serving as his inspiration. If he accepts Ivan's plan for escape, might he be rejecting his own salvation?

Dmitri seeks help and explains to Alyosha that Ivan has planned the escape because he believes Dmitri to be guilty. Alyosha reassures his brother that he never believed him to be the murderer. Alyosha then searches for Ivan and finds that he is on the verge of a mental breakdown.

During the first of Ivan's interviews with Smerdyakov, Ivan is told by the cook that he ran away because he already knew that violence was readying itself in the Karamazov house and Smerdyakov further reminds Ivan that the two of them are very much alike. Neither of these ideas Ivan accepts, but he broods on them and as he leaves he feels that there is "an insulting significance in Smerdyakov's last words." It is this ambiguity that brings him back for a second interview.

During this next interview, Smerdyakov accuses Ivan outright of desiring his father's death. "You had a foreboding," he says, "yet went away." This was, in effect, Ivan's open invitation for Smerdyakov to murder Fyodor. Ivan recoils and threatens to expose Smerdyakov to the police, but the servant is wily. He reminds Ivan that he also will be disgraced in the public eye and will be accused of being an accomplice. Ivan realizes the possibility of the cook's threat and slowly concedes that he is indeed guilty. Literally, technically, Smerdyakov is the murderer, but he, Ivan, must share the guilt. This realization weighs heavily on Ivan and before long he is driven to despair. Then he reads the letter that Dmitri has written Katerina telling of his plans to murder his father and is even more confused. His anxiety finally subsides, but he cannot be sure now that Smerdyakov murdered Fyodor. He returns for a third interview.

Now both Ivan and Smerdyakov are ill and no longer talk in riddles. Smerdyakov openly tells Ivan, "You murdered him; you are the real murderer; I was only your instrument, your faithful servant, and it was following your words I did it." Smerdyakov also reminds Ivan of the philosophy that "everything is lawful if there is no immortality" and that Ivan consented by going away. "By your consent to leave, you silently sanctioned doing it," he says. Ivan still cannot accept Smerdyakov as the murderer, however; as the facts stand, he is guilty, *even* if the servant did commit the deed.

Ivan faces his own conscience that night in the form of a tormenting devil. The doppleganger is a witty, urbane, and clever aberration. He affirms nothing for the distraught Ivan and at Ivan's every question, he merely asks another, often ridiculing Ivan's most private fears.

At the end of Book XI, Alyosha arrives with the news of Smerdyakov's death but Ivan is little concerned with the cook's fate. The realization of his own guilt has so shamed and confused him that realities have almost wholly dissolved.

BOOK XII

Summary

The day of Dmitri's trial arrives and the courtroom is filled with curious visitors from distant parts of the land; the trial has aroused much interest. Besides the gruesome details of parricide, which will be discussed, Dmitri is being defended by the celebrated criminal lawyer, Fetyukovitch, who has come from Moscow to undertake the defense and, it is noted, the jury is made up of mostly peasants. Can such country people understand the subtleties of the much-discussed case?

Dmitri enters the courtroom exquisitely dressed in a new frock coat. The judge then reads the indictment against him and asks for his plea. Dmitri responds, "I plead guilty to drunkenness and dissipation... to idleness and debauchery... but I am not guilty of the death of that old man...." Most of the people in the courtroom, however, even those who are partial to Dmitri, believe that the case against him is a strong one, for much of the evidence and nearly all of the witnesses' statements seem to indicate Dmitri's guilt.

Fetyukovitch is an exceptionally skilled trial lawyer. He has grasped all the various aspects of the case and as Grigory, Rakitin, Captain Snegiryov, the innkeeper from Mokroe, and others are called to testify, he skillfully discredits the testimony of each of them, pointing out inconsistencies in their statements and creating doubts about the integrity of their motives.

Later, when three medical experts are called to testify about Dmitri's mental state, each doctor suggests a different cause for Dmitri's behavior and thus, with the medical evidence so contradictory, there is no firm support for either the prosecution or the defense. There is a minor exception, however; the local doctor, Herzenstube, tells several interesting stories about Dmitri's childhood and creates some new sympathy among the listeners.

Alyosha proves to be an asset for his brother because he is well known for his integrity, and during his testimony, he is able to recall an incident with Dmitri, one that happened just before the murder. It proves that Dmitri did have a large sum of money on him and that he did not murder Fyodor for the 3,000 rubles. This fact impresses most people and convinces them that Dmitri has not stolen old Karamazov's secret fund.

Following Alyosha in the witness stand is Katerina, who tells of Dmitri's saving her father from ruin and then refraining from black-mailing and thereby seducing her. Her story is heard with mixed inter-est, but Dmitri feels that she need not have told the tale because it is a severe blow to her integrity. Now it is publicly known how thoroughly she has humiliated herself for Dmitri. Grushenka is able to add little to Dmitri's defense except for her passionate outcries that he is innocent.

Ivan has not yet testified. His testimony has been postponed be-cause of his illness but suddenly he appears at the trial and at first he is unable to speak sense. He can give no evidence. Then, as he is about to leave, he turns and shows the court the 3,000 rubles that Smerdyakov gave him. He reveals that Smerdyakov is the murderer and that he al-lowed the servant to perform the act. He becomes so excited that he says that he has a witness for everything he has said — a devil who visits him at night. Hysterically, he asserts the truth of his testimony but is finally dragged from the courtroom, screaming incoherently.

The trial has one more surprise before it recesses. Katerina reverses her statements and shows the court the letter that Dmitri wrote, stating that he might be forced to kill his father. She defends Ivan because she knows that he is suffering from mental illness. Grushenka then accuses Katerina of being a serpent and an uproar follows. When order is finally restored, the lawyers give their concluding speeches.

Once more, Kirillovitch, the prosecutor, describes the murder and analyzes the members of the Karamazov family, emphasizing Dmitri's passionate and undisciplined personality and reviewing in detail Dmitri's activities and his statements during the days preceding to the murder. He insists that Dmitri is exactly the sort of man whose violent disposition would drive him to seek a solution to all his problems through crime. Kirillovitch then dismisses Ivan's theory that Smerdya-kov is the murderer by pointing out that the servant did not have any of the qualities of a murderer's personality; he had no motive and, fur-ther, was incapacitated on the night of the crime. Dmitri, on the other hand, did have a motive — his hatred for his father — and he had a great need for money. All this, plus the letter he wrote to Katerina, says the prosecutor, is conclusive proof that the crime was premeditated and was, in fact, committed by Dmitri Karamazov. He concludes by making a stirring appeal to the jury to uphold the sacred principles of justice and the moral foundation on which Russian civilization is built by pun-ishing this most horrible of all crimes — the murder of a father by his son.

Fetyukovitch begins his defense by emphasizing that all evidence against Dmitri is circumstantial. No fact withstands objective criticism if examined separately. He also points out that there is no real proof that a robbery took place; the belief that Fyodor kept 3,000 rubles, he says, is only based on hearsay and there is no reason to disbelieve Dmitri's explanation of where the money he spent at Mokroe came from. He also reminds the jury that the letter Dmitri wrote to Katerina was the result of extreme drunkenness and despair and cannot be equated with premeditated murder. Then, after reviewing all the evidence, he makes this final and important point: Fyodor's murder was not that of parricide. The man was never a father to Dmitri, nor was he a father to any of his sons. It is true that Fyodor's sensuousness resulted in Dmitri's birth, but Fyodor was a father in that respect only. After Dmitri was born, Fyodor continually mistreated the boy and from then on, neglected all his parental duties. He, in fact, abandoned the boy. All his life Dmitri endured mistreatment and now, if he is convicted, the jury will be destroying his only chance to reform and to make a decent life for himself. The lawyer asks for mercy so that Dmitri can be redeemed. He reminds the jury that the end of Russian justice is not to punish. Rather, it is pronounced so that a criminal can be helped toward salvation and regeneration.

The audience is overcome with sympathy and enthusiasm and breaks into applause. The jury retires. The general consensus is that Dmitri will surely be acquitted but such is not the case. When the verdict is read, Dmitri is found guilty on every count.

Commentary

Recorded in detail, in this book, is Dmitri's trial and here is massive evidence of Dostoevsky's long interest in the proceedings of the Russian courts and of the psychology practiced by lawyers. Dmitri's attorney, Fetyukovitch, for example, is able to undermine and cleverly discredit the testimony of every witness. He is particularly masterful as he points out that Grigory, unused to drinking, had been imbibing on the night of the murder and could have seen "the gates of heaven open up." Likewise, with all witnesses, Fetyukovitch discovers and enlarges a loophole in their statements so that truth becomes extremely tenuous.

The trial, which up to a certain point has been shaped by the incisive intelligence of Dmitri's lawyer, takes on a new turn as Ivan comes forward to give his testimony. He desires to tell all he knows and to confess his own part in the murder but he rages incoherently and, most of all, finally suffers a nervous collapse. This, in turn, forces Katerina to admit evidence that ultimately convicts Dmitri. The confused young girl, in her attempt to save Ivan from disgrace, produces the letter written by Dmitri announcing his plan to murder his father, if necessary, to pay back the money he owes. More than any other factor, this letter condemns Dmitri.

The final section of Book XII covers the long speeches of the prosecutor and the defense attorney in which each summarizes the arguments of the trial and offers his interpretation. Actually, nothing new is revealed in these speeches. They serve chiefly to illustrate the nature of the legal minds emerging in Russia during this period.

EPILOGUE

Summary

After Dmitri's trial, Alyosha goes to Katerina's, where Ivan is ill, unconscious, and burning with high fever; in spite of gossip, Katerina has ordered that he be brought to her house. When Alyosha arrives, she confesses her deep regret over what she revealed during the trial, but says that already Dmitri's escape is being planned. She explains further that more help is needed; Alyosha must aid his brother and bribe the appropriate officials. Alyosha agrees, but forces Katerina to promise that she will visit Dmitri in prison.

Alyosha then goes to his brother and tells him that Katerina will also come, but Dmitri has weightier problems troubling him. He explains his craving desire to repent and, through suffering, to become a new human being. He fears only one thing: that he will be unable to carry out his intentions if the authorities do not let Grushenka accompany him. Alyosha explains the plans that have been made for the escape and, reluctantly, Dmitri agrees to them. He makes one stipulation, however; he escapes only for the present. Someday he must return to Mother Russia.

Katerina then enters and she and Dmitri ask each other for forgiveness. Peace though is not so easy, even now, for Grushenka unexpectedly arrives and although Katerina begs her for forgiveness, Grushenka still feels too bitter toward her former rival to acknowledge any pleas.

Meantime, little Ilusha has died and Alyosha leaves Dmitri to go to the young boy's funeral. After the burial, Alyosha talks with the many school friends of Ilusha and asks them to remember forever their friendship at the present moment. He, in turn, promises that he will never forget any one of them. The boys are deeply affected by Alyosha's sincerity and all cheer, "Hurrah for Karamazov."

Commentary

In a sense, the epilogue conforms to the nineteenth-century custom of tidying up the end of a novel. Here the final fates of all characters are revealed and the reader is relieved from any speculating. Dmitri accepts Ivan's plan for escape, but only after he has Alyosha's sanction. As for Alyosha, he conforms to the directives of the late Father Zossima. He does not condemn his brother nor does he object to the escape. In short, he refuses to judge Dmitri.

Even in his escape, it is important to note that Dmitri feels that he will suffer immensely. He has been depicted as being closely attached to Russia and to be exiled to America—to be separated from the soil from which he takes his strength—this is an extreme form of punishment for him. His plans are to return to his country as soon as possible and then to live anonymously in some remote region. This lasting love for Russian soil, of course, reflects Dostoevsky's passion for his native land.

In the novel's final pages, all concern is with Alyosha and the young school friends of Ilusha. The ex-monk has had little success with adults in Russian society, but with children he is unexcelled. The boys eagerly gather around Alyosha and are openly responsive to his speech about love and devotion—a message quite clear: Dostoevsky believes that youth, nurtured on the wisdom of Father Zossima, will be the salvation of Russia.

CHARACTER ANALYSES

FYODOR KARAMAZOV

The father of the Karamazov brothers is a disgusting sensualist. He has virtually no redeeming qualities. He is a self-centered man—corrupt and immoral—and is cynically dedicated only to the fulfillment of his bestial appetites. He has married twice for selfish reasons and has treated each wife with total disrespect. Little wonder, however, for a man who has no respect for himself can respect no one else.

As pointed out during Dmitri's trial, he was never, in the truest sense, a father to any of his sons. When they were young, he was oblivious of their presence and relieved when relatives took them away. Later, he refused to give any of them money, and although the matter is not stated definitely in the novel, all indications suggest that he cheated Dmitri out of a large portion of his mother's inheritance.

Fyodor's vulgarity is part and parcel of his every action; he lives the part of the vulgar buffoon, delighting in embarrassing anyone who is in his presence. Not unsurprisingly, his degeneration leads indirectly to his death; it was his seduction of the village idiot, "stinking Lizaveta," which produced Smerdyakov, the strange epileptic who grew up as his father's servant, then dispassionately slaughtered him.

DMITRI

Dmitri, the oldest Karamazov son, and the only son who grows up with the expectation of coming into property, can be considered the pivotal figure of the novel. The novel revolves around his guilt, in connection with the murder of Fyodor Karamazov, and Dmitri is the person who undergoes the most significant change during the course of the novel.

Dmitri does not have the intellectual pretensions of Ivan and cannot understand his brother's metaphysical concerns, nor is Dmitri as spiritual as his brother Alyosha, although he basically accepts God and immortality. He is, in fact, best represented as being caught midway between a sort of "Madonna-Sodom" opposition; he fluctuates between two poles of existence. Coursing through him are impulses for honor and nobility, side by side with impulses toward the low and the animal. This duality is partly explained by Dostoevsky's belief that the typical Russian is able to love God even while he sins. Dmitri, for example, declares that he will love God forever, even if God sends him to hell.

A particularly crucial scene and one that shows Dmitri's contradictory personality is his manipulation of events in order to force Katerina to come to his room so that he can seduce her. When she arrives, Dmitri cannot carry out his scheme. The better part of his nature has gained control of him.

Compounding Dmitri's confusion is his realization of being raked by these polar extremes. He says, at one point, that "beauty is a terrible and awful thing," meaning that a beautiful woman can arouse sensual desires, yet can also, and at the same time, inspire noble and elevated thoughts. He is the victim of opposite extremes of passion yet cannot comprehend their origin, their dimensions, or their purpose.

When Dmitri is cornered with a serious accusation, of which he is innocent, he begins to face the consequences of all his past acts. Up to now he has lived with no regard for consequence. He has spent money without discretion and has bragged about his intention to rob his father; now his character is forced to change. And it is after his interrogation that he begins to emerge as a tragic figure. He realizes that his past life is not free of guilt and duplicity and, although he is innocent of his father's murder, he is willing to accept another's punishment. This suffering will reform his life and for the first time there exists genuine hope for his resurrection.

IVAN

Ivan's basic nature is defined early in the novel when he is depicted as being a very independent child. He is, in contrast to his brother Alyosha (who freely accepts help and aid from other people), unable to receive freely any act of generosity.

By nature Ivan is a very studious person who has strong intellectual inclinations, qualities that later completely dominate his personality. As a result, we come to know Ivan through his thoughts rather than through his actions; in other words, his intellect defines his essential nature.

As an adult, Ivan seldom speaks and then only to individuals who seemingly are intellectually capable of understanding his complexities. When he accompanies the others to the monastery, for instance, he is quiet and reserved; he waits to talk until someone begins to discuss Ivan's article, written while he was still at the university. This article is a key to Ivan's makeup; he is an atheist, yet concerned with the fate of mankind on this earth; all of his studies have led him to a deep compassion for the sufferings and tribulations of earthly man. But he cannot, honestly, accept religious matters on faith alone. That which does not conform with human logic is totally unacceptable to him. Unlike Alyosha, he cannot accept the abstract theory of God's mercy and goodness because he has seen too many examples of injustice and suffering in the world. He refrains from questioning the existence of God, but refuses to accept this world as being God's world. Ivan feels that a God who is infinitely good and just should have created a world where there was no innocent suffering. Nor can he accept the idea that all innocent suffering is a part of a great plan because God gave unto man a human mind and any theory concerning God's justice must be understood by this God-given mind. Sadly, logic cannot explain the long history of human suffering.

From his questionings, then, Ivan has developed a long prose poem entitled, "The Grand Inquisitor," in which he envisions Christ returning to earth. He is again threatened with death, but this time He is indicted by the church. Christ's second death is demanded because the cardinal explains that mankind is too debased to accept the ideas advocated by Christ. The church, consequently, has taken away the freedom that Christ promised man and for man's good, it has enslaved him. In this poem, Ivan reveals the depths of his compassion for mankind, creatures who he feels do not have the strength to follow the strenuous demands made by Christ.

Ivan supports a general acceptance of Christian morality because he feels that if the average man does not have some type of dictate to follow that an era of lawlessness ensues. Faith in immortality and a healthy fear of retribution are great deterrents to crime, Ivan believes, for with no immortality, then logically "anything is allowed." And it is this statement which Ivan expresses to the servant Smerdyakov that leads to the murder of Fyodor Karamazov. Smerdyakov, convinced that anything is permissible if there is no divine retribution, feels free to commit any act; he chooses parricide.

ALYOSHA

The youngest son of Fyodor Karamazov embodies most of the positive actions in the novel. From his early years onward, we learn that he was an easy-going youth whom everyone seemed to love. Unlike his brother Ivan, he is totally unconcerned with accepting charity or gifts from others. Dostoevsky depicts him as the sort who would quickly give away any money that he might possess.

Alyosha is no stock Christ-figure, however; of all the so-called good characters in Dostoevsky's fiction, Alyosha seems to breathe the most life. This is partly due to the fact that he constantly moves among people and performs quiet acts of kindness and love, even though he is not always successful.

When we first meet Alyosha, he is a member of the monastery and a special disciple of the religious elder, Father Zossima. And, as the story progresses, he becomes the living embodiment of all of Zossima's teachings. Every action of his reflects the qualities that he learned from his elder. For example, he refuses to condemn, he has an unusual ability to love all, and he has great faith in the basic goodness of man.

Alyosha, however, did not come to this faith easily. His credibility as a character is equated with his struggles to keep from losing his belief in God's justice. Particularly after Zossima dies, he questions a God that would allow such a holy man as Zossima to be disgraced by a rotting corpse, putrid and repulsive to his mourners. He rejects a justice that would dishonor a noble man for no logical reason. Then, after Alyosha begins his questionings, he is tempted away from his monastic vows by eating forbidden food, drinking vodka, and being induced to visit Grushenka, reputedly a sensuous, loose-moraled young woman. After the visit, however, Alyosha discovers the great power of all that Zossima has preached. He feels deep compassion for Grushenka and because he refuses to condemn her, he restores her belief in herself and in others. And, more important, Alyosha rediscovers his own faith in all its encompassing magnitude.

Adding to Alyosha's credibility is his failure to convince adults of Zossima's message. His role is not that of an all-perfect, all-successful young missionary. He has his share of failures. His successes, though, are therefore all the more important. In particular, his dealings with young boys are remarkable. He treats them as equals and they respond as equals, and we are led to believe that Alyosha will preach and lecture and that Russia will learn young Karamazov's wisdom. Thereupon, Dostoevsky seems to be saying, the destiny of the country will be the result of Alyosha's message of faith and love.

GRUSHENKA

By the end of Dostoevsky's long novel, Grushenka comes to represent the Slavophillic Russian Woman. She is the female counterpart of Dmitri, the personification of the ideal Russian, whose typical beauty does not immediately attract attention.

When she is first introduced, it is true that she is capricious and willful, but she has suffered a desertion by her former lover, and has finally made herself financially independent so that she can be a "free-spirit."

Grushenka's change of character begins with her captivating both father and son in the Karamazov family. As a coquette and as a tease, she dangles both men and causes them to become bitterly jealous of each other. When she realizes the consequence of her irresponsible nature, however, she assumes her share in the guilt surrounding Fyodor's murder. Perhaps one of her greatest values lies in her faithfulness. As she had previously been true to her first lover, when she finally realizes her love for Dmitri, she vows to remain forever constant and faithful to him. Furthermore, she also accepts her involvement with the murder and willingly seeks to share the guilt with Dmitri. All these factors help redeem her in spite of all her capricious past.

CHRONOLOGICAL CHART

DAY BEFORE MURDER

ALYOSHA	IVAN	DMITRI
Leaves the monastery. Visits his father, goes to see Katerina, meets the boys, and is bitten by Ilusha.	Goes to Madame Hohlakov's house in order to talk with Katerina.	Goes to Samsonov's to borrow money. Is sent by Samsonov to see Lyagavy (Gorstkin).
Goes to Katerina's house and talks with Madame Hohlakov and Lise. Upstairs, he tries to unite Ivan and Katerina.	Explains his position and love for Katerina in Alyosha's presence. Leaves to look for Dmitri.	Pawns watch and borrows money from landlady.
Is sent by Katerina to Captain Snegiryov's house with money; learns Ilusha's identity.		Travels to neighboring town to find Lyagavy.
Returns to Madame Hohlakov's house; finds Katerina in hysterics. Leaves to find Dmitri.		Finds the priest who tells him that Lyagavy is some miles out in the country.
Hears from Smerdyakov that Ivan is in a restaurant waiting for Dmitri.	Leaves message with Smerdyakov for Dmitri to meet him in the restaurant.	Walks the miles to find Lyagavy.
Goes to the restaurant, discusses the idea of suffering with Ivan and hears Ivan recite the poem on the Grand Inquisitor.	Calls to Alyosha to join him in the restaurant. Discusses God, immortality, and the idea of innocent suffering; recites his poem on the Grand Inquisitor to Alyosha.	Arrives at the cabin of a forester. Finds Lyagavy drunk.
Returns to the monastery and listens all night to Father Zossima's last words.	Returns home but cannot sleep before 2 A.M.	Sleeps at the cabin in the hope of borrowing money from Lyagavy when he wakes and sobers up.

DAY OF THE MURDER

ALYOSHA	IVAN	DMITRI
After talking all night, Zossima dies early in the morning and Alyosha remains with the elder's body.	Awakens at 7 A.M. and begins to pack. Tells Fyodor that he will tend to some of his father's business in the neighboring town.	Awakens to find Lyagavy drinking again. Gives up hope and seeks transportation back to town.
At 2 P.M., the body begins to smell, Alyosha is in despair.	At 2 P.M., he catches a carriage to take him to the train station. Before leaving, he tells Smerdyakov of his change in plans.	
Rakitin discovers Alyosha and tempts him.		Arrives in town; takes Grushenka to Samsonov's. Pawns his pistols with Perhotin.
Alyosha agrees to go to Grushenka's house.		
He arrives at Grushenka's and hears of her ex-lover's return.	Arrives at the train station.	Goes to Madame Hohlakov's to borrow money from her. Has his futile talk with Madame Hohlakov and leaves her. Encounters Samsonov's servant, who tells him that Grushenka did not stay at Samsonov's house.
Watches Grushenka leave to join her ex-lover.		Sees Fenya (Grushenka's servant), who pretends not to know where Grushenka is. Rushes to Karamazov's house; sees his father. Tries to leave and is hindered by old Grigory. Strikes the servant aside and returns to Grushenka's house.
	Catches the train.	
Alyosha returns to the monastery.		
At the monastery, he has the dream of the wedding in Cana and also undergoes his mystical experience.	On the train, Ivan calls himself a wretch for leaving as he did.	Redeems pistols and orders food and wine, and heads for Mokroe.

REVIEW QUESTIONS

1. Compare the basic differences in the personalities and philosophies of Alyosha, Ivan, and Dmitri.

2. State briefly Fyodor Karamazov's personality and indicate his relationship with each of his three sons.

3. How does Fyodor's relationship with Smerdyakov differ from his relationship with his legitimate sons?

4. What influence does Ivan have upon Smerdyakov? What is Ivan's relationship to his other brothers?

5. How does Ivan's story of the Grand Inquisitor relate to his general views throughout the novel?

6. How is Ivan's concern for suffering humanity related to his story of freedom and security in the "Grand Inquisitor" section?

7. Compare the philosophical views advanced by Ivan with those maintained by Father Zossima.

8. How is Alyosha an embodiment of Father Zossima's teachings?

9. Write an essay justifying Dmitri as the main character of the novel.

10. How is Dmitri's repentance and desire for suffering and regeneration a reflection of Zossima's teachings?

11. Contrast the roles and personalities of Grushenka and Katerina.

12. How does Alyosha's relations with the young boys function in the total scheme of the novel?

SELECTED BIBLIOGRAPHY

BERDYAEV, NICHOLAS. *Dostoevsky: An Interpretation.* New York: Meridian, 1957. Berdyaev uses *The Brothers Karamazov* to show that it is the culmination of all of Dostoevsky's ideas. He relates each idea to an earlier expression in previous works.

CARR, EDWARD HALLET. *Dostoevsky, 1821-1881: A New Biography.* New York: Macmillan, 1949. Carr sees *The Brothers Karamazov* as Dostoevsky's first active proclamation of his faith to the world. In this novel, Dostoevsky has worked out to his satisfaction the link between sin and suffering and has resolved the conflict between faith and reason. Carr also treats the religious, romantic, and masochistic elements that formed Dostoevsky's doctrine of suffering.

GIDE, ANDRE. *Dostoevsky.* New York: New Directions, 1926. By selecting illustrative passages from his works, Gide discusses various ideas appearing in Dostoevsky's works and also explores the superman idea which pervades much of Dostoevsky's writings. The volume is perhaps most important as an expression of a great twentieth-century writer about a great nineteenth-century writer.

GIFFORD, HENRY. *The Hero in His Time: A Theme in Russian Literature.* New York: St. Martins, 1950. Gifford relates Dostoevsky's "heroes" to the typical movements and ideas during Dostoevsky's times.

IVANOV, VYACHESLAV. *Freedom and the Tragic Life: A Study in Dostoevsky.* New York: Noonday, 1952. Ivanov uses the "Grand Inquisitor" section as a focal point in explaining Dostoevsky's views about freedom and security.

LAVRIN, JANKO. *Dostoevsky.* New York: Van Nostrand, 1947.

MAGARSHACK, DAVID. *Dostoevsky.* New York: Harcourt, 1963. Magarshack presents a very readable account of Dostoevsky's life, but makes little or no effort to interpret the artistic achievements.

MIRSKY, DMITRI. *History of Russian Literature.* New York: Harcourt, 1963.

PACHMUSS, TEMIRA. *Dostoevsky: Dualism and Synthesis of the Human Soul.* Carbondale, Ill.: Southern Illinois University Press, 1963.

REEVE, F. D. *The Russian Novel.* New York: McGraw Hill, 1966. Reeve has an excellent section discussing the problems confronting Ivan and relates Ivan's ideas to the conflicts faced by Dostoevsky.

SEDURO, VASSILY. *Dostoevsky in Russian Literary Criticism.* New York: Columbia University Press, 1957.

SIMMONS, ERNEST J. *Dostoevsky: The Making of a Novelist.* London: Oxford Press, 1950. Mr. Simmons' book is perhaps the best treatment of Dostoevsky found in English. He sees *The Brothers Karamazov* as an expression of Dostoevsky's ideas and illustrates how each character functions as an embodiment of an idea.

Stravogin's Confession with a Psychological Analysis of the Author by Sigmund Freud, ed. VIRGINIA WOOLF and S. S. KOTELIANSKY. New York: Lear Publishers, 1949. The interest in this lies in Freud's psychological analysis of Dostoevsky.

WASIOLEK, EDWARD. *The Brothers Karamazov and the Critics.* San Francisco: Wadsworth, 1967.

WELLEK, RENE (ed.). *Dostoevsky: A Collection of Critical Essays.* New York, Prentice Hall, 1962.

YARMOLINSKY, AVRAHM. *Dostoevsky, a Life.* New York: Criterion, 1934. An interpretative analysis of Dostoevsky's novels in relation to his life.

NOTES

NOTES

NOTES